ACCELERATED SUCCESS

How One Woman Built a $4 Million Home Business in 20 Months!

How One Woman Built a $4 Million Home Business in 20 Months!

Donna Reid-Mitchell

2007 Women of Enterprise Award Recipient

accelerateddsuccess.reidmitchel@gmail.com

Foreword by Evertrue Bell

Accelerated Success
How One Woman Built a $4 Million Home Business in 20 Months!

First Edition

This publication is designed to provide general information in regard to the subject matter covered. However, laws and practices often vary from state to state and are subject to change. Because each factual situation is different, specific advice should be tailored to the particular circumstances. For this reason, the reader is advised to consult with his or her own advisor regarding their specific situation.

The author and publisher have taken reasonable precautions in the preparation of this book and believe the facts presented in the book are accurate as of the date it was written. However, neither the author nor publisher specifically disclaim any liability resulting from the use or application of the information contained in this book and the information is not intended to serve as legal, financial or other professional advice related to individual situations.

It is sold with the understanding that the publisher is not engaged in rendering legal, accounting, or other professional service. If legal advice or other expert assistance is required, the services of a competent professional person should be sought.

Published by:
Donna Reid-Mitchell
Frisco, Texas
acceleratedsuccess.reidmitchel@gmail.com

Cover design and inside layout: TheBookProducer.com
Accelerated Success Cycle© illustration: Jacqueline Blake
Editor: Lauri Dodd

Printed in the United States of America

ISBN: 978-0-9817828-0-5

DEDICATION

We all need someone or something to stimulate us to be our best and for me that motivation came from my son Yordan and my daughter Rhiannon. They have bigger dreams and goals than I do, and they keep checking to see if I am getting A's at work as I expect them to get A's at school. This book is dedicated to my children for their inspiration and support in my pursuit of excellence. A special debt of gratitude goes to my mother for the love and guidance she has given me throughout my life. She is my true role model.

ACKNOWLEDGMENTS

I believe that our success in life is largely determined by the company we keep. I want to thank everyone who has helped me along the way, especially the following people: First, thanks to my parents for instilling spiritual values early in my life that I still hold near and dear in my heart. A lot of who I am and who I will become has been greatly influenced by my seven siblings: Sonia, Marjorie, Ini, Joan, Rose, Delou and Keisha.

Special thanks go to Heather Harewood who first introduced me to the awesome Avon opportunity and told me with conviction that I, too, could be one of Avon's best.

I have been influenced, supported and coached by some outstanding individuals, my upline, Peter and Bernadett Calamaras, Maria Rivera, John Fleming, Juan Cabrera, Evertrue Bell, Vondell McKenzie, Maxine Sullivan, Michelle Merriwether, Maria Peninger, Garth Warner, Donna Miles, Teresa Ficara, Lisa Truett and Marlyn Reyes who all encouraged me to work at being a successful entrepreneur.

My downline represents an awesome team of incredible business partners. I respect your commitment and thank all of you for your invaluable partnerships. To my Senior and Executive Unit Leaders your success is my success, I am sending a special thanks to Marjorie and Recardo Sharpe, Suzan Williams, Michelle Edwards, Tanesha Farquharson and Maria Smith.

Thanks to all of my fellow Avon Representatives who do so much daily to make the Avon opportunity the best in the industry. We have come a long way together, as the new professional network marketers.

Thanks to all who have shared in person, through emails or phone contacts that you have been inspired in some way by my Avon story, a special thanks to Evertrue Bell who told me I had a story worth sharing and Gladys Drever, District Manager in Canada who told me I needed to write a book, now I have…

I wish you all accelerated success!

Donna Reid-Mitchell
Avon Senior Executive Unit Leader

Contents

"The No. 1 thing people can do to increase their wealth is to start a part-time business."

– Robert Kiyosaki

* * *

"Network marketing has proven itself to be a viable and rewarding source of income."

– Donald Trump

FOREWORD

I heard the name Donna Reid-Mitchell for more than two years before I had the great pleasure of meeting Donna in the summer of 2006. The words used to describe Donna at the time, were that "She's a great Sales Leader." "She's incredible and a gracious person; she has really figured out this business of network marketing." While all of these statements are true, they only scratch the surface of who Donna really is.

Another pleasure was spending eleven days in Jamaica working with Donna and Juan Cabrera, Donna's Division Sales Manager at the time, to re-energize an already successful sales organization. I was able to observe the two of them interact with individuals who had serious goals and dreams. The two weeks on the island working with Donna and her team validated how important it is to seek out the "right" leaders to establish partnerships to build a solid network marketing business. I have worked with many successful people throughout my 30 years in the direct sales and network marketing industries. However, I place Donna at the front of the pack as an exceptional leader. Our time together was spent assessing the four critical skills (prospecting, appointing, training and developing other leaders) of Donna's key business partners.

What was amazing is that Donna's genuine interest in helping her team achieve success was unlike any I had seen. She selected 10 high potential leaders to meet with us individually so that we could conduct accelerated 90-day business planning sessions, and did she choose the right individuals? Yes. How do I know that? Well each of the leaders she chose came to the business planning sessions with two or three of their best people. In fact one came with five from her downline. She apologized for bringing them without an invitation, but she wanted them to share in the business planning session with her. Now how often does that happen? Over the course of the two weeks we connected with more than 20 of Donna's serious business partners, who all wanted more out of life.

I thought to myself, "This lady has the ability to influence and empower others!" Donna was already successful when I met her thanks to her upline leaders. The economic environment had changed since Donna started in the industry, and she was willing and ready to try some new strategies to help her team accelerate their performance.

She knew they needed help visualizing the true potential of the business opportunity. They also needed specific facts on how many lives have been changed by those who are passionate about this business of relationships. Donna will share how she expanded her team's belief in how they could work part time as home-based business owners and earn as much or more than they were earning working full time for someone else.

This book is about how one individual—Donna, who took on the challenge to prove that network marketing works, when you work the business. More than 15 million Americans and more than 53 million people worldwide worked as independent direct sellers and network marketers in 2007, and they sold $30.8 billion worth of products and services. The numbers translate into one out of eight U.S. households today are earning from a home-based business. At the time of this writing, $90 billion in worldwide sales are being generated by individuals who are partnering with companies that offer high quality and unique products direct to consumers. "The direct selling channel is strong and the numbers are expected to climb as the economy recovers," said Neil Offen, the Direct Sales Association President and CEO. "Most importantly, direct selling continues to offer millions of Americans an excellent source of supplemental income, which is particularly important in a questionable economy."

Donna's story is about how she started part time, shifted to full time at her own pace, and how she went on to build a substantial income selling beauty and personal care products from her home. Donna will share how she found a company that provided all of the business tools she needed to run a successful business from her home in the same fashion as large corporations. Donna already had an innate ability to influence people, and with the hands-on training and guidance she received, she was able to accelerate her personal performance, while at the same time partnering with her serious Sales Leaders to teach them to do the same.

Donna's book became a labor of love as she received countless calls and emails requesting copies of her calendar and copies of the speeches that she has shared from the stage. It soon became clear that it was far more than a book, but a journal that captured her personal steps and triumphs on how she built a $4.2 million business in 20 short months. This book illustrates how strong her network of powerful leaders is and how amazing people are from all around the world. It wasn't until Donna was asked to share her story that she realized how powerful she, too, was at developing other leaders.

Within these covers, you'll read stories of people Donna inspired to accelerate their personal performances. It has happened over and over again, and it can happen for you, as well. In the end, it's the repetitive nature of how Donna shares her story that will cause you to retain the important message of the need to commit to a specific success cycle for one to two years so you can re-set your goals and dreams and take control of your life as Donna has.

I know Donna's journey will touch you as much as it has touched me and many others. If you are in network marketing, you will be inspired to take your business to the next level. If you are not in network marketing, the book will shed some light on the fascinating network marketing industry. Network marketing provides a great income equalizer—it empowers people from all educational, social, ethnic and financial backgrounds to build a thriving business from their homes. You can build a business as big as your ability to dream. Network marketing is more than a business, it's an industry that has changed millions of people's lifestyles in record breaking time.

Let this book change your small dreams into BIG Dreams!

Evertrue Bell
Certified Network Marketer, Global Trainer
Fayetteville, North Carolina

Dear Readers,

This ***Accelerated Success*** journal is being provided to address the many requests that I have received to share my story about how I achieved success so quickly with my home-based business.

If you are reading this journal, it's because you have demonstrated in some way that you have the ability to dream. Either through your expressions or actions, you have made it known that you are ready to take responsibility for your future. The key to attaining your dreams is as simple as making a commitment to a specific success cycle that you can and will work with for the next one to two years. Achieving success is not easy; if it were, everyone would be living his or her dreams, today. This journal will help you accelerate your success because you will find an abundance of strategies that you can immediately use to improve your skills as a leader. Becoming an exceptional leader is the ticket to financial freedom, which leads to empowerment and a better life. So…before we get started, what are your current dreams for yourself and your family? List three specific short-term dreams that you want to achieve for yourself and your family in the next 90 days to six months.

Personal Dreams	By When	Family Dreams	By When

Great! By writing down your short-term goals you are demonstrating that you have the ability to dream. Most adults have lost their ability to dream; many of us settle for what life provides us, often never even challenging life's gifts. Women especially spend the majority of their lives as caregivers: taking care of the family, spouses, parents, grandchildren, work, and siblings. Being a caregiver is a good thing; however, it may cause you to put your personal dreams in a permanent holding pattern.

If you haven't written any short-term dreams in the space above, go back and do it. Write something whimsical like pampering yourself with a full-body Swedish massage to relax and de-stress, or treat yourself to a fine dinner at a great restaurant that you've always wanted to go to, even if you have to go alone. Plan to spend at least $100 on yourself for a five-course meal: you deserve it. Suze Orman, the famous financial advisor, often shares with her clients that "they deserve success; it's their birthright." I believe that, and I want you to believe that you can achieve each of the goals and dreams you listed above and much more.

"Since it doesn't cost a dime to dream,
you'll never short change yourself
when you stretch your imagination."

– Dr. Robert Schuller,
Minister, Author

ACCELERATED SUCCESS CYCLE©

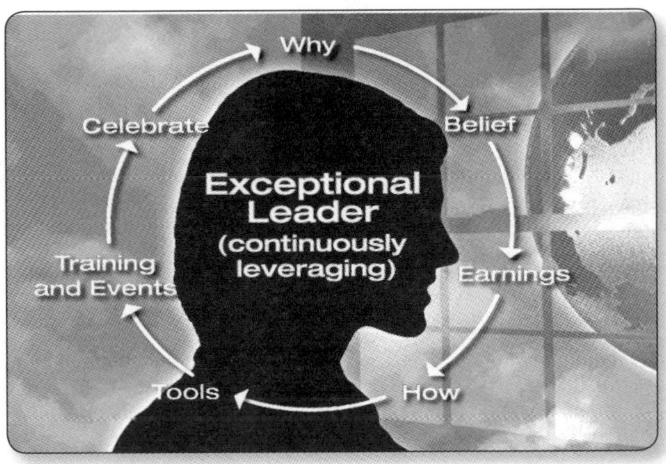

Because of the many hours of personal coaching and training that I have received, I have become a much stronger leader. Now I want to share what I have learned to help others developed the attributes of an exceptional leader, too. I received coaching and training from some of the best leaders in the direct sales and network marketing industry, and together we captured my early successes and the success of many of my downline members as illustrated in this ***Accelerated Success Cycle©***.

This journal is about how I used the above cycle to regain control of my life. After suddenly becoming a single mom of two young children, I used this cycle to help me turn a devastating divorce into a $4 million dollar home-based business in 20 short months. I will share how I took control of my situation and made a conscious decision to not just survive, but to excel. Starting with a short-term goal made it easier for me to feel like a winner. Within a short time I was achieving significant life-changing dreams as the sole supporter of my family by selling lipsticks and bubble baths.

You will learn about the ***Accelerated Success Cycle***© and how you, too, can use it to build an incredible home-based business. As you read my story, I will be taking you through the cycle several times so you can understand how I achieved my dreams and goals in 20 short months.

To benefit from my journey, focus on these three key areas:

❖ How can you ***accelerate your personal actions*** to improve the quality of your family's lives through a home-based business? If I can build a $4.2 million business in less than two years, so can you.

❖ Learn and use the seven steps of my ***Accelerated Success Cycle***© to change your life as it has changed mine and many of my incredible business partners.

❖ Start immediately to "***Make it Happen***" for yourself and at least 10 other serious leaders. Zig Ziglar said, "We will get everything we want when we help enough others get what they want."

As you take this journey, try to identify the many times I changed my dreams during the two years that I worked to achieve Senior Executive Unit Leader at Avon. I learned that I had to continuously change my dreams to match my desire to create a better life for my family. To stay focused, you, too, will want clear and defined short-term and long-term goals that have great meaning to you. Starting a business is easy, but achieving significant success requires a dream and a commitment. Let's begin the journey together….

If You Want Happiness

If you want happiness for an hour –
take a nap.
If you want happiness for a day –
go fishing.
If you want happiness for a month –
get married.
If you want happiness for a year –
inherit a fortune.
If you want happiness for a lifetime –
help others.

– Chinese Proverb

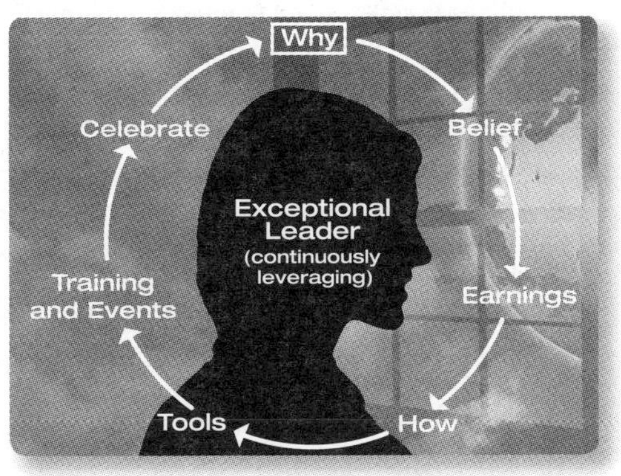

Step 1 – Why

Why build a home-based business?

I was blessed as a child growing up in Jamaica to have a mother who played an active role in our lives. I have six sisters and one brother. One of my fondest memories is of my mother, a stay-at-home mom who never worked; the time she gave us is something that I have always treasured. My early memories of my mom instilled in me the desire to own a home-based business.

My husband was already living and working in the United States and in 2001 I left Jamaica to join him with my five-year-old son Yordan, a year later my daughter Rhiannon was born. My husband was taking care of all of our family expenses, and I was working long hours as a hair stylist, while selling Avon part time primarily to my salon customers.

Then, to my surprise, shortly after moving to the U.S., my marriage fell apart, and I found myself in an overwhelming position as a single mom with the full responsibility of raising two small children. As I saw it at the time, my choices were to become homeless in New York, or return to Jamaica. I didn't want to do either.... I knew I had to take control of my life because I was now a single mother. The three of us were living in a one-bedroom apartment in New Rochelle, New York.—our living standards had changed, and I knew that I wanted more for my children. In fact, it was my son, Yordan, who helped me see that we could have a brighter future.

One evening after complaining about the long hours I was spending at the beauty salon, and the struggles of finding dependable childcare, and trying to find time to service my Avon customers, Yordan said, "Mommy, you are the best Avon Lady I know, and I am going to help you." That was a pivotal moment in my life. I decided right then and there to change how I viewed the world, and what's amazing is that it took a 6- year-old to show me a new vision.

"It's scary to change your life.
But a great career should fit into your life,
not the other way around.
At least give your ***dream*** *a chance."*

– Shana Spooner

At the time, I worked full time in a beauty salon as a hairstylist, and I was doing well. I had a strong and loyal clientele, and I truly enjoyed being a professional cosmetologist. That was my passion. At that point in my life, I never saw pursuing any other career as an option.

I enjoyed the relationships I had with my clients and, most importantly, being my own boss. Any hairstylist today can tell you that you only earn an income when you are "behind the chair." So after having my daughter, I decided that I wanted to spend some time at home with her, because putting her in day care at 8 weeks old was not an appealing option.

I started looking for an easier earning opportunity, which led me to signing up with Mary Kay and Avon at the same time to see what both had to offer. I paid the $10.00 start-up fee for Avon and $100 fee for Mary Kay. I also purchased Mary Kay's $600 stock up opportunity. Remember, I was not looking for anything complicated that would require too much time since my main priorities were my 6-year-old son and my baby. For the first three months I can honestly say that I was my own biggest customer. I was shopping for myself, my baby, my son, my mother and my house.

I chose Avon because I didn't have to do evening parties and I could take Yordan and Rhiannon out with me to do the business—after all, it was Yordan's idea for us to work the business. I started selling beauty and personal care products five years ago as a direct seller with the grand goal of earning $100 a month. Ladies and gentlemen, I can proudly tell you that I exceeded my first goal.

Denzel Washington, actor and director of the movie The Great Debaters, used this important phrase in the movie that his real mother had often said to him – "Do what you have to, so later you can do what you want to." I learned that to become an exceptional leader I had to follow Denzel's mothers' instructions—to work hard now so that I can enjoy my children and my life more fully later. I started my journey by clarifying my "why," which was to provide a comfortable lifestyle for my children. At that time, I decided to make a two to three year commitment to work on building a successful home business.

Stop here and determine your "why."

Why do you deserve success?

____

____

What will you be able to do for yourself and/or your family when your earnings from your home business exceed $1,000 a month?

____

____

Are you willing to learn how to work the business as other exceptional leaders have learned to do?

____

____

How do you like to learn? Reading, listening to audios, attending seminars, workshops....

____

____

How will you celebrate when your business exceeds the first $100,000 in total business sales?

____

____

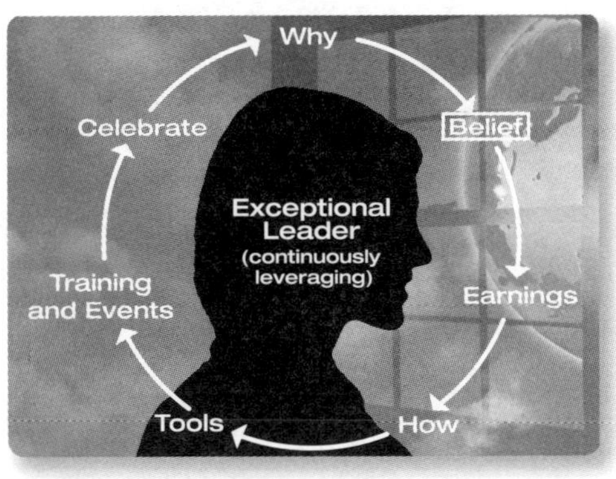

Step 2 – Belief

Believe you deserve success

At the first Avon meeting I attended, my manager showed excerpts from Avon's *Women in the Spotlight* DVD. The DVD has 11 inspirational stories of women who had developed multi-million dollar home-based businesses. Each one had risen from unusual circumstances to incredible heights.

I was fascinated by the Representatives featured—their stories and the lifestyles they had attained; it was then for the first time I realized that Avon was a real career opportunity, and it offered the potential to make substantial earnings. When I saw the stories on the DVD, I was going through the toughest time of my life.

Although I had a 6-year-old son and an 8-month-old baby to care for, I had made the decision to divorce my husband. While I knew it was the right thing to do, the stories on the DVD helped me to realize that others had overcome their challenges, and they gave me the confidence that I could, too.

I talked my manager into lending me the DVD, and for the next week I watched the DVD every day, OVER AND OVER. I learned… no, I *memorized* all eight of the stories. Each one touched me in a special way. VONDELL MCKENZIE resides in California, she is a beautiful and elegant woman who started her Avon business in her fifties. She started building her Avon business with her husband who was ill at the time. Together they worked to become Avon's first successful network marketing team, becoming the first to earn the Senior Executive Unit Leaders title in the early 90s.

Vondell remains today one of my most admired peers. She's graceful and very willing to share what she has learned about this business. I strive everyday to be like her when I "grow up." In fact, it was Vondell that inspired me to accelerate my personal performance to the Senior Executive Unit Leader level.

As I listened to her story I thought, "Wow… she built her seven-million dollar business before the Internet, before Avon offered online training and all of the incredible business tools and support we enjoy today, and even without an upline!" Vondell's business now generates over $13 million-dollars a year and is still growing.

Vondell's first goal in 1990 was to buy a few new business suits; she was able to do that rather quickly. Her next goal was to buy a luxury car. The first car she purchased was a 1992 Cadillac Sedan Deville. Her first long-term goal was to build a new home. She wanted to build her new home with her Avon office in the front. In 1997, Vondell was showing off her new home in Avon's first *Rich and Famous* DVD. As planned, her home had enough space to run her business; she had ample space for training and to have small meetings with her downline. The structure of her home allows her to separate her personal life from her business. This really appealed to me because at the time, my Avon business was wrapped around me and my two children in a very small one-bedroom apartment in New York. Vondell's next goal was to purchase another luxury car, a Jaguar, which she was able to do in 2001.

What she said that I most connected with was that she loved being her own boss. She loved setting her own goals, and being able to set her own pace. Most importantly, she said she loved being in control of her own schedule. She shared that when she went to France, she didn't have to ask anyone if she could take off. She simply drew a line through her appointment book and said—"I am not here."

I also connected with the inspiration she received from her parents. Vondell's mother taught her the importance of taking control of her life. Her father told her that you have to know what you want and you have to go after it… he said, "Just because you may be down at the moment, you don't have to stay down." Even today, she credits her father with instilling in her the desire to set and achieve goals.

Vondell said that when she first learned about Avon's earnings opportunity, she believed that she could earn a very good living, which would allow her to live differently than she was currently living. That was the clincher.

On the DVD she asked a series of questions, and I felt like she was talking directly to me. In fact, since my son was at school, and Rhiannon was too young to know that I was talking to myself… I answered each one of those questions aloud—with conviction and confidence, as if we were both in the same room.

Vondell asked me:

- "What is it you really want?
- If money were no issue, where would you want to go; where would you travel?

- If money were no issue, in what type of house would you live?
- What kind of car would you drive?
- What would you give?
- What would you do for your children?
- Where would you send them to college?"

She told me that I could be anything I wanted to be... and I immediately saw myself as a Senior Executive Unit Leader just like her.

PEARL HEILBUT, another Senior Executive Unit Leader from California was also featured on the DVD. At the time, Pearl had been with Avon for 23 years. She spoke of the security that Avon affords her and the friendship and joy she got from helping others succeed. What touched me most about Pearl was that she wanted to stay home with her children. I was extremely impressed with what her children said about her, and how her decision to be a work-at-home mom affected them.

Her daughter, Dottie, said, "Our mom is the most driven woman you will ever meet. She outdoes all of us; I thank her for the drive she instilled in us to achieve our goals in life. And she was there for us—I thank her for that." Pearl's son, Craig, said his mom's hard work "got him where he is today." He also said that for his mom, her children are her reward, and "what makes her successful is seeing her kids succeed in life." Pearl's sister, Gwen Rowly, said that Pearl is very focused and passionate, and they all admire her for being there for them.

I wanted my children to feel that way about me. I wanted to be the "rock" that Pearl's children had found her to be.

I also connected with Pearl when she spoke about earning awards. She said prior to joining Avon she was a legal secretary and she had never earned any awards or recognition. In the next moment, the camera revealed a striking baby grand piano and book shelves where she proudly displayed all of her beautiful district, division and national awards.

She shared that she was most proud of the national awards earned by ranking in the top five in the United States out of more than 600,000 Avon Representatives. I thought, "Wow… I don't have any awards either." At such a low point in my own life, I was feeling vulnerable that maybe I had let my children down by making the decision to divorce their dad. They love him dearly, and I knew I had to not only regain their confidence in me, but I also needed to prove to myself that I was a winner as well.

I wanted to experience the things Pearl had with Avon. She said Avon made her feel like a queen! And because Avon felt more like a family to her, there was never a time she thought she *wouldn't* succeed in her business. That really got my attention.

LISA WILBER's segment of the video started with her saying that in 11 years in the business, she had already earned a total of $1.2 million! I thought, "Oh my goodness! I must rewind the video. Did I hear her correctly?" Lisa was the first one to talk about her earnings. Up to that point, others had only spoken about the total sales generated from their entire downline which was also impressive.

But now I was sitting up and really listening. I had so many questions for Lisa, and once again, I spoke directly to the TV. "How many years did it take you to earn a million? What is your background? How did you do it?"

Vondell and Pearl had both spoken about walking their neighborhoods to find customers, but then Lisa shared a different method of attracting customers and recruits. She ran ads in the classified section of the newspaper. Now I am taking notes, saying, "I can do this!"

I also connected with Lisa on another level as well. Her husband had been the one to inspire her to succeed. She had just been laid off from her job as a secretary earning $20,000 a year. She was depressed and crying about losing her job, when her husband said, "Honey, why don't you do more with your Avon business?" My son, Yordan, had encouraged me in the same way, saying that I was the best Avon Lady he knew, and why didn't I expand my Avon Business? I realized then that my support system at home could help cheer me on to the same level of success in Avon that Lisa had achieved.

I ran to get my calculator and I figured out that Lisa's earnings had doubled almost five times in 11 years. I thought that even if I worked as a hairstylist for another 30 years, my earnings would never increase at that rate, and I couldn't bear to think of all the hours I would have been away from my children to be that successful as a hairstylist.

I heard Lisa say that in 1992, her first year as a Sales Leader, she earned $5,000 and she invested all of it back into the business. I immediately popped out the DVD to see that it had been produced in 2003. So with my trusted old calculator I went to work again on her numbers… and what I discovered from her message was that in the year the DVD was made—just over a decade after her layoff, she had earned $230,000! And she projected that for 2004 she was on track to earn $250,000, which was a $20,000 increase in earnings in just one year!

I sat there thinking about Lisa being laid off from a job where she earned $20,000 total for a full year of work—her boss had actually done her a favor by laying her off! Today, in 2008, if Lisa continued to increase her earnings by $20,000 a year, she's probably earning more than $300,000 now. From those numbers, I figured that Lisa had been increasing her earnings by 8-10% every year. I had been a hairstylist for 11 years and it was very difficult to increase the salon prices. Although I had a loyal clientele, it wasn't industry standard to raise salon prices every year—even though the cost of doing business in the salon continued to increase.

By now, I was sitting on the edge of my chair in my tiny New York apartment thinking, "Are these women real?" I was getting more excited by the minute about the Avon opportunity. From that day, because of what I learned from Lisa, I started tracking my earnings and my progress every quarter. I am so grateful to Lisa for sharing her life-changing numbers.

MIKI CROWL, Senior Executive Unit Leader from Iowa started her story by saying that her Avon business expanded as her two girls grew. She also shared that when they went off to college, her business exploded. Miki talked about how she was earning $600 a month from Avon's car allowance program in addition to her bi-weekly network marketing check and her earnings from product sales. I thought, "My… that's three income streams from one home-based business!"

And if that wasn't enough to get me fired up, she said she was able to buy two brand new cars for both of her daughters when they went off to college. When Miki's daughter, Jacklyn, talked about how Miki pulled her and her sister in a red wagon down the street to help her put Avon brochures on the doors, I was ready to cry, wondering how this DVD could be so focused on me. I looked at my baby, Rhiannon, and told her, "Today I have found our family business."

Miki said her first check was $8, and now she receives checks every two weeks for more than $5,000. I thought, "That's $10,000 a month plus her $600 car allowance… I thought…our lives would be very different with that kind of money."

MALCOLM and MARY SHELTON, Senior Executive Unit Leaders from Indiana were number seven on the list of *Avon's Rich and Famous* achievers. What impressed me most about their story was when Malcolm elaborated on the network marketing concept. He talked about Avon's program that allowed people to earn money by sponsoring people, and those people to earn by sponsoring people, and so on. I didn't know much about network marketing at that time, but he was talking about building a downline and all the benefits that came with it. And I knew he was describing the way that Lisa's income had grown so rapidly.

To fast track their success, Malcolm and Mary had recruited 100 people to their team in the first 90 days in Avon. They said their business had doubled and then tripled over the past 10 years. They had done so well, in fact, that Mary had been able to leave her job as a school teacher after they had worked their Avon business for only four short years.

I was touched as I listened to Mary talk about the time she and Malcolm were out delivering Avon products in a nice tree-lined neighborhood, and she was wondering if they would ever be able to afford to live in an up-scaled neighborhood like that. Their hard work had paid off, because within a decade, they were living in the home of their dreams.

It was obvious that the Sheltons understood network marketing. They had compared Avon to other companies and they spoke the language. While Mary brought up the statistic that 70% of the people in the U.S. are not connected to an Avon Lady, Malcolm highlighted the fact that every five years their earnings would double.

This was a language that I wasn't accustomed to hearing. But I was really learning to like the sound of the business. Before I saw the DVD, I had never heard anyone talk about

Avon in that way. I learned so much from the Sheltons' story. In fact, after hearing that they had given their downline a named, I decided right then to form a team and call it "The Island Achievers." Then I got to work quickly, because Malcolm had inspired me to recruit 100 people in 90 days just as they did… and I have been earning as a serious network marketer ever since.

JACKIE and DAN MUNDY were very humble. They talked about how they had nearly lost their car, right about the time they were forming their dream to open their own Avon training center. Jackie's first goal was to buy a new refrigerator, which they were able to do very quickly. And I was amazed to hear that a short time afterward, they were also able to purchase a new home to put their appliance in as well! I really felt that Dan was talking to me when he said that "the best time to join Avon is now."

After watching and listening to these stories over and over, I started to dream bigger. It was at this point that I decided to build a million-dollar network marketing business like all of these awesome leaders. These are just a few of the many success stories at Avon. They all affected me deeply. I wanted the success that they were enjoying.

I have to go back to the story on the DVD that made the greatest impact on me—Vondell McKenzie's. Her story was even more amazing, because she became Avon's first Senior Executive Unit Leader before technology, professional tools or role models were really in place for her to follow. In addition to all of that, she had lost her husband, who had been her lifelong business partner. Vondell and her husband built their business on belief. She was introduced to the business by someone she respected and trusted, John Fleming, an industry expert and one of Avon's corporate leaders.

John offered the McKenzies the business opportunity, and he instilled in them that they could build a six-figure business from their home. They never challenged the plan or the process; they simply changed their dreams and subsequently significantly changed their lives. Today, 17 years later, Vondell continues to perform as one of Avon's top Senior Executive Unit Leaders, leading a team of more than 2,000 Avon Representatives. She's now enjoying the benefits from a $13 million home-based business. Just imagine the kind of life Vondell would have had as a widow if she hadn't believed in herself and the opportunity that had been presented to her and her husband.

At a recent Avon training session, the trainer said that one McDonald's restaurant would have to sell 75,000 Big Mac combo meals in a two-week time frame to match the sales that Vondell's downline generates in two weeks. WOW… what a business! Many of us allow our fears to overpower our beliefs and therefore never take the first step to achieve our dreams. Even today, I encourage the use of tools like Avon's *Rich and Famous* and the *Women in the Spotlight* DVDs with my downline, because those tools left a bigger impression with me than anything that was said at the time I joined Avon.

With a renewed belief in my abilities to be the next Vondell McKenzie, I increased my brochure orders from 10 to 200 a campaign, and I started putting recruiting flyers in all of the brochures. I set a goal of five new recruits every two weeks. Yes, there were days when I got tired and discouraged, but I made a conscious decision to let my **efforts** rise above my excuses because my desire to succeed was greater than my will to quit.

My Avon business was doing well from the product sales side; I had achieved President's Club in my first year with very little effort. I had sold more than $10,000 in consumable products. I found it easy to attract customers with samples and brochures. The key was adding customers every day through face-to-face contacts and referrals. The people I met were already Avon customers and they knew what they wanted. I just had to provide regular and consistent service.

In my experience, selling Avon was easy, and after two years of building a strong customer base, I decided to expand my business as a network marketer. Although I had never managed or led anyone before, I had the past successes to guide me. I wanted to be like Vondell, and she made it look so simple and immensely rewarding, that I changed my belief again and started to truly visualize myself as the next Senior Executive Unit Leader.

The biggest challenge I was experiencing with my downline members up to that point was getting my part-time Representatives to become serious business builders. Their current Avon earnings were not enough to keep them motivated. That was when I realized I had to change how I was working with my leaders.

I stopped and reflected on all of the coaching and feedback that I had received from the many people who had helped me achieve success thus far. What I began to understand was that I needed to put myself and my serious leaders on an "accelerated plan" to achieve greater success, faster.

My second "Aha!" moment happened when I attended my first Looking for Leaders training session in May 2006. The workshop helped me to see that I could really achieve consistent success. It covered everything we needed to help us move our business from good to great. It was structured, fact-based, and measurable. The workshop helped us look at the strengths, weaknesses, and the awesome opportunities our business offered.

I learned at the workshop that we had to review and plan our business in 90-day segments. First, we needed to set goals for a three-month period, review our results, and then set goals to maximize the four quarters of every year. I had never thought of the business that way.

In the past, I had focused only on the two-week cycle, and I wasn't getting everything done. Planning my business over 90-days instead, allowed me to add balance and manage my business in a more professional manner. I got the concept that night and I immediately told all my Unit Leaders who had attended the session that it was imperative for us to meet to conduct their individual 90-day business planning sessions, ASAP.

I wanted them to have the same benefit that I had experienced when Juan Cabrerra, my former Avon Division Manager, and Avon's national training manager, Evertrue Bell, exposed me to the new way of analyzing my business. I shared with my leaders that after my first 90-day business planning session, which took place just prior to the workshop, I saw many areas that I could focus on to achieve immediate results in increasing my earnings, and I wanted to share what I had learned with each of them. I let them know I had learned a new way to look at the business as a serious network marketer, and I was sure I could help them increase their earnings right away.

We all got so excited that the same night, after the three-hour Looking for Leaders workshop, I met with several of my future Executives to conduct their 90-day planning sessions to help them accelerate their success. And because we took immediate action to apply what we learned at the workshop, it has resulted in a more productive and profitable experience for all of us. After I clarified my "why" and increased my belief that I could be an exceptional leader, my personal earnings not only increased: my earnings exploded in the following six months.

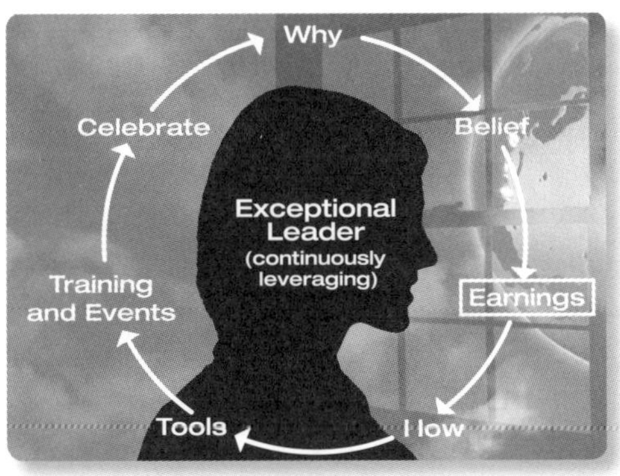

Step 3 – Earnings

When did my earnings explode?

I earned my title as Senior Executive Unit Leader rather quickly, and after learning how to review the critical elements of my business, I felt more confident as a leader. I was no longer embarrassed about revealing the results of my business. Because I am now working my business consistently, I am a role-model armed with specific facts about my business that I was proud to share. The results that I had achieved are now new benchmarks for my downline. I encourage them to "beat" my performance. Because I was able to achieve SEUL in 20 months, I am now looking for someone on my team to do it in 18 months.

My earnings exploded when I started to focus on helping my team members advance their titles in 90-days. As a result of this focus, my business had grown so fast that I had not taken the time to think about how I got to $4.2 million so quickly. And to tell you the truth, I didn't know what to look for, or how to put my successes in a format that would inspire others.

I was somewhat surprised at my success. However, my mentors helped me to understand what I had done well. I had established some business standards that I could proudly transfer to my team of my serious Unit Leaders. From the first minute I watched the DVD, I immediately took massive actions to advance my business unit and as a result, my earnings truly exploded. The chart below demonstrates how every time my title changed my earnings doubled.

My First Five Years as a Network Marketer

2003	2004	2005	2006	2007
C22 New Unit Leader	C3 Executive Unit Leader	C9 Senior Executive Unit Leader	C26 Senior Executive Unit Leader	C15 Senior Executive Unit Leader
$62.15*	**$1,201***	**$2,672***	**$6,101***	**$8,065***
2 Campaigns	7 Campaigns	40 Campaigns	The journey to SEUL took 20 months, and my life has truly changed!	

* A "campaign" equals a two-week selling and earnings cycle.
* Your earnings and results may vary.

I achieved Unit Leader in two campaigns, and my first network marketing check in 2003 was $62.15. I was so excited to receive my first check. Especially after hearing Miki Crowl say her first check was $8.00. Receiving that check was the confirmation that I was on my way to something great. I skipped from Unit Leader to Executive Unit Leader in campaign three of 2004, achieving Executive Unit Leader in seven campaigns.

My check for two weeks increased to $1,201 in three short months. This was 18 times more than I had earned as a Unit Leader: explosive! I was gaining momentum, and my love for this business was increasing by the day.

In campaign nine of 2005, just short of 20 months, or 40 campaigns of really working my business, my title changed to Senior Executive Unit Leader, Avon's highest earnings level, and my earnings tripled, again.

As you can see from the chart, my earnings truly exploded, because I took the time to develop more serious business partners. I am now enjoying earnings that are well over $10,000 a month, and I am on my way to being the next Vondell McKenzie. All of my early dreams have now become a reality—things like being able to choose my neighborhood so that my children can be in a better school district. We now live in a beautiful home that not only has space for my family but for my Avon business as well.

I am able to balance my business and personal life, and I feel confident that I will continue to achieve my new goals because I have learned how to help others accelerate their performance even faster than I did.

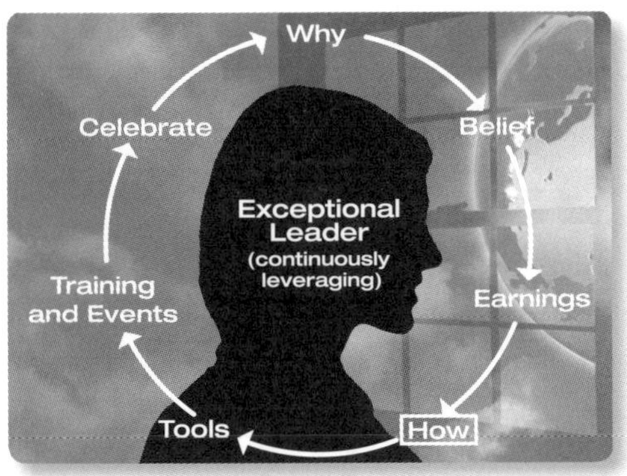

Step 4 – How

How do you develop a million-dollar business?

My business has grown so fast that I was concerned about how I was going to keep it going. However, having my first 90-day business planning session with my mentors showed me that it was possible to continue growing, as you can see from the previous chart. I learned that my business partners and I had to focus more on the three Ps of our business and not just the standard activities like getting our customers' orders processed, but more on increasing every business unit in my downline's overall productivity.

Learning about the three Ps was a big eye opener for me. The first "P" is about ***Products***: I was taught how to take control of the total product growth of my downline—because if I don't teach my downline to sell, they will never increase their teams' sales volume from $1,200 to $40,000 per campaign to enable them to achieve earnings as Senior Executive Unit Leader like me. One of the things I learned to do that was so simple but powerful was to review my downline members' invoices with them to help them determine what they were selling most. I found out that my team was focused on taking orders on the fixed earning products (20% items) like shoes and purses 90% of the time instead of selling the benefits of the consumable products.

I immediately changed how I trained my new recruits. Now I teach them to use the brochure as a top seller would, as opposed to settling on being just an order taker. I also shared with my Unit Leaders that we had to take responsibility for our downline members that quit because they were not earning enough. It was our responsibility to teach them to sell, and we had to focus on each one of our new recruits for the first three months, showing them how to sell personal care, skin care and more consumable products so that they can earn up to 50% commissions—consistently.

The results were amazing. With this focus alone, my team promoted 48 titles in the last 90 days of 2006. My team earned the prestigious honor of leading the nation in the fourth quarter title advancement incentive. The recognition was great, but what was most meaningful was that Avon rewarded the strongest leaders on my team with $17,500 in additional bonus earnings from that incredible incentive.*

Eight of my Executive and Senior Executive Unit Leaders, and I received bonuses that ranged between $500 and $4,500 in addition to our regular earnings from our product sales and our downlines' commissions. This was the turnaround. My leaders are now making real money, and they were eager to teach what they had learned to their downline members. By focusing on the first "P," products, we are now winning. At the close of 2007, my total unit sales continued to grow to $4.9 million. We finished the year with an $800,000 sales increase in a difficult economy.*

My goal for 2007 was for my unit to generate $5 million in total unit sales in my fifth year. We missed it by $52,000. But I am proud of the $4.9 million and I have no doubts that we will exceed the $5 million in 2008.*

The second "P" of network marketing is all about the ***People.***

The first part of my business turnaround started with me. I realized that I was stagnant and not consistent, and yet I wanted my team to be consistent. So I decided that I had to do what I was expecting them to do. In C10, 2006, I had 103 active 1st generation downline members and I personally increased my team to a high of 146 active downline members. The new recruits in my downline increased from around 40 per campaign to another high of 97 new recruits in a two-week campaign… due to a team of highly motivated business partners. I was now leading by example. I know you have heard that statement, but it is true… we have to do what we expect our leaders to do.

Every week now, I try to conduct three or four business planning sessions by phone or in person. We work on getting commitments on title advancements every 90 days, which was a new concept for all of us, and now I tell all my downline members it is not only encouraged but expected. I knew my downline members, but I had never really used the Avon Downline Manager's genealogy tools to really understand how I could help my leaders go from being good to great. This was one of the most rewarding parts of my personal business development.

Some of my team members had just been too busy with careers, school and family to dream. Others had just gotten complacent and content with their earnings. So we have been partnering more with their respective uplines to inspire and motivate them to want more and to dream bigger.

---

* Your results may vary.

Two of the business development sessions that I did, in particular, really stand out in my mind. The first was a 19-year-old Advanced Unit Leader, and college student: Rushane Sterling. I helped him move from Advanced Unit Leader to Executive Unit Leader in less than 90 days, primarily by transferring what I had learned about the three Ps.

When I reflect on his story, I realize how this process has duplicated itself for Rushane and his downline. This was another pivotal moment in my career, because I knew I could help others accelerate their own success just as I had. When I looked at my Downline Manager reports for Rushane at the close of campaign 15, 2006, to plan his ***Accelerated Success Cycle***© follow-up session, it was amazing to see the progress he continued to make. Both his personal sales and unit sales were up. He had developed five more Unit Leaders for a total of eight, securing his Executive Unit Leader status.

Because of the time Rushane's upline and I spent discussing his business development opportunities, he is recruiting more consistently, and he earned his largest check to date in campaign 15, 2007 at $1,582*. Rushane gave himself a 187% increase in earnings in less than 90 days! His journey to success is interesting when you consider he took what he learned and helped others achieve phenomenal success as well.

At the time, with the encouragement of his upline and District Manager, Rushane and one of his downline members, Abigail Ward, were in a friendly competition to see who would achieve Senior Executive Unit Leader first. Well, Abigail crossed the finish line first, earning the SEUL title in campaign 14, 2008—and running close behind, Rushane advanced

* Your earnings may vary.

to SEUL in the very next campaign. Interestingly, Abigail's momentum encouraged Rushane to strive harder to achieve his own goals.

We all are proud of both Rushane and Abigail, and I am extremely proud of Rushane and what he has accomplished. The amazing thing about how this business works is that although he's only 21-years-old, a year from now, not only will he be earning a substantial amount from his own efforts, he will also be earning from Abigail's million dollar home-based business as well. It really drives home the saying that a rising tide floats all boats.

The second ***Accelerated Success Cycle***© of which I am extremely proud is Michelle Edwards. She was a former taxi driver, who attended her first Looking for Leaders workshop, and went on in the next campaign to personally recruit 12 new team members. Michelle earned her Fast Start Bonus in C14, 2006, and her personal earnings doubled four times in her first year as she pursued the title of Executive Unit Leader. Michelle achieved Executive Unit Leader in C8, this year… in just 9 months. Michelle put ***herself*** on an accelerated success plan.

All of my Unit Leaders have committed now to leading by example and to be professional in attire and business dealings at all times so that they can attract like- minded people to their team. I teach them to see every new recruit as their next Senior Executive Unit Leader. I shared that we all have to be tough on ourselves to succeed and consistently sell, share, show, and watch carefully to make sure that our new recruits far surpass our removals every campaign.

I stress with everyone that when we get the first 2 "Ps" right—selling products and developing our people—the third "P," which stands for ***Profits***, will automatically come… and that is just what has happened for all of us. We all are working to improve the quality and dedication of all new recruits by asking for a six-month commitment at the time of appointment.

We are targeting more men and couples because of the proven success rates of those groups in the network marketing industry. We are targeting more professionals in addition to looking for "work-from-home moms." We all are now enrolling in professional organizations and networking more with entrepreneurs. The 90-day business planning sessions have helped all my Unit Leaders see more clearly the value of their business units over a six-campaign period.

Mrs. Field's Recipe for Success:

Love what you're doing.

Believe in your product.

Select good people.

-- Debbi Fields

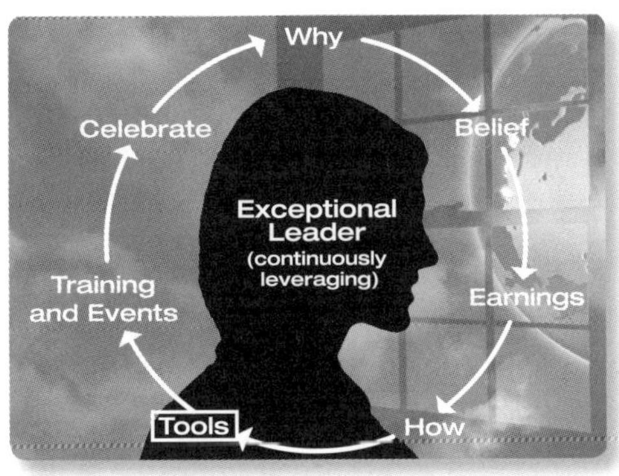

Step 5 – Tools

TOOLS THAT CHANGED MY BEHAVIORS

During my business review discussion, I realized I had to work a 90-day calendar to make sure I stayed on top of my business. Let me share some of the steps I have taken now that I am working my business as a network marketer. I realized that the first thing I needed was to get an assistant to delegate some of the tasks I was previously doing myself on a daily basis. I wanted to spend more time **DEVELOPING LEADERS,** and because my business had grown so quickly, to more than $4.2 million dollars in less than two years, I could no longer do everything myself.

I set out to find a bi-lingual assistant so that she would be able to communicate both verbally and in writing with all the members of my downline. I then wrote down all the tasks I did daily that were business related, and I identified all the things that I needed to do personally and separated what I could delegate to my assistant. Avon's Downline Manager Business tool makes it easy for me to use an assistant to help me with the development of my Downline members and the management of all the administrative things we must do.

Using an assistant also required me to use a calendar. So I started creating 90-day calendars that contain all of my personal and business appointments. Take a look at my calendar before I achieved Senior Executive Unit Leader. I spent an average of nine hours a day in the beauty salon and worked my business in the evenings and Sundays through Tuesday, leaving little time for my family and worship.

I had no real plan or strategy. I was all over the place trying to do everything myself, and I was always putting out a lot of fires. My days were very predictable and they didn't focus on my goal of achieving Senior Executive Unit Leader.

My Weekly Calendar *Before* I Achieved Senior Executive Unit Leader

Day	Weekly Activity/Task
Mon	Prospecting for customers & recruits
Tues	Prospecting for customers & recruits
Wed	Beauty salon 9 am – 6 pm Evening appointment & deliveries
Thurs	Beauty salon 9 am – 6 pm Evening appointment & deliveries
Fri	Beauty salon 9 am – 6 pm Evening appointment & deliveries
Sat	Beauty salon 9 am – 6 pm Evening appointment & deliveries
Sun	Product deliveries and prospecting at community events

My Weekly Calendar *After* Becoming Senior Executive Unit Leader

Day	Weekly Activity/Task
Mon	Conference calls with all 1st generation Unit Leaders and above. Review last week's accomplishments & set new weekly agenda with key Unit Leaders
Tues	Establish downline development contacts: Confirm admin. activities: call no-orders, mail books, share selling tips, develop customers list and prospect for 2 hours
Wed	Call new Representatives; conduct training contacts. Conduct Development Seminars, workshops, Opportunity meeting or Success Hours to grow units.
Thurs	Review titles at risk/select 3 top sellers to convert to Sales Leadership
Fri	Balance removals with new appointments. Make customer deliveries and prospect for four hours.
Sat	Complete 2 classes or audio sessions per month for personal development
Sun	Worship & kids day

I have now created a primary mission for each day of the week. Setting these daily objectives keeps me focused and consistent. Yes, there are interruptions and surprises that pop up, but I adjust when needed and get back to my daily missions as soon as I can. I also develop my calendar in 90-day segments to make sure I allow balance in my life. Making this change helped me tremendously, and in two short years I was able to start working my Avon Business full time. Planning this way allows me time to focus on the three "Ps" while building relationships with my serious business partners.

Here's a quick overview of what my days are like, now. More details will be covered later. From 6 to 7 a.m. I check my emails and review the Downline Reports. I look for memorable moments that I can use to inspire my leaders, and I identify those that need support or encouragement.

At 7 a.m. I get my son up and out to school. I am in my office at 9 a.m. working on my daily scheduled activities. Mondays, I am on the phone starting at 8 a.m. making calls to my first generation titled downline members, and they are invited to include any of their titled downline members to join us on the conference calls. This is usually my longest work day but one of my most rewarding days as well.

On Tuesdays my first call is to my business assistant to plan her week. She now does all my mailings, which include a welcome package to new representatives, sharing selling tips with those ordering under $100, sending current brochures, and sharing the current offers to members without orders. She follows up with all new recruits with less than three months of experience. I try to schedule three or four telephone 90-day business planning sessions between 10 a.m. and 2 p.m., and I go prospecting until 4:45 p.m. when my son gets home from school.

Wednesdays, I get a list from my assistant on all the new Representatives I need to follow up with, and this is the day I do my follow-up training contacts for the new recruits and development contacts for those who are building units. Wednesday is also my training day to develop my current and new Unit Leaders. I partner with my Executive and Senior Unit Leaders to schedule opportunity presentations, Leadership Development Seminars, Looking for Leaders workshops, and Success Hours every month. We rotate the sessions monthly in different areas and support each other with attendees at every event.

We have found that these sessions are providing us with a constant stream of people to work with for title advancements. We tell them that the prerequisite for attending is that they must have **"THE DESIRE, the DISCLIPINE AND THE DEDICATION TO DEVELOP A SUCCESSFUL BUSINESS."** This way, they know we have high expectations from the outset. This approach has resulted in creating more fast starts and more Unit Leaders on their way to becoming Advanced Unit Leaders.

Thursdays, I call and email my leaders who are at risk of losing their titles. In addition to sending e-cards and email, I like to follow up with a phone call, as I get better results by talking personally to my leaders. Fridays, I am usually in the field doing appointments, prospecting with my team, and delivering customer orders.

I train my new downline members to do a minimum of three things every day to advance their business. For those who have a desire to achieve Executive Unit Leader or higher, I encourage them to complete ten or more of what we call "accelerated actions" every day to build their business to the Senior level, faster. (See Accelerated Actions on page 64.)

Now I share my Accelerated Personal Action Planning calendars with my leaders and encourage them to use it as a guide in setting their personal and business agendas as each individual situation varies. I try to pack my days as much as I can because when my son gets home from school, I switch to the "mommy mode" until I put both my son and my daughter to bed at 9 p.m. Then I work in my home office for another hour or so as needed. "I am committed to doing what I need to do today, so that I can do what I want to do five to 10 years from now."

Until you value yourself,
you won't value your time.
Until you value your time,
you will not do anything with it.

– M. Scott Peck

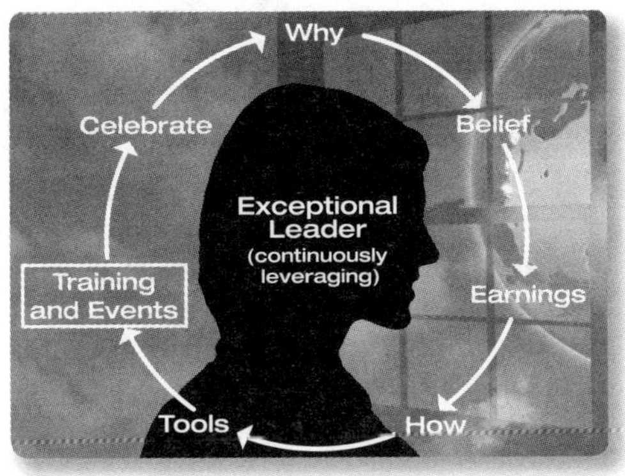

Step 6 – Training & Events

Training and Events Are Critical to Your Success

Our great company keeps making it easy for us to grow our business. My team and I now look at every Avon event as an opportunity to excite and train our business partners. When Avon offers a new incentive, we schedule an "emergency" meeting with all of our Executives & Seniors to make sure everyone understands the opportunity and to make sure they understand that it is a limited offer. I challenge my top leaders to see who can develop the most ***new*** Unit Leaders during every incentive timeframe.

In fact, twice in the last year my team finished 1st in the nation in title advancements. As I shared earlier, we helped 38 titles change in the last three months of 2006. Then again in the first three months of 2007, we helped 48 more Representatives advance to the next level in a short 90-day period. We maximized every event and training session to help those 86 new Representatives see how they could change their dreams in order to change their lives. We are making dreams come true faster now! We are all committed to learning so that we take advantage of Avon's training and support. We go to all of the events, no matter where they are located or what the cost.

All of the training events help us to look at our business units as network marketers. And the events have given us the confidence that we can continue to drive forward.

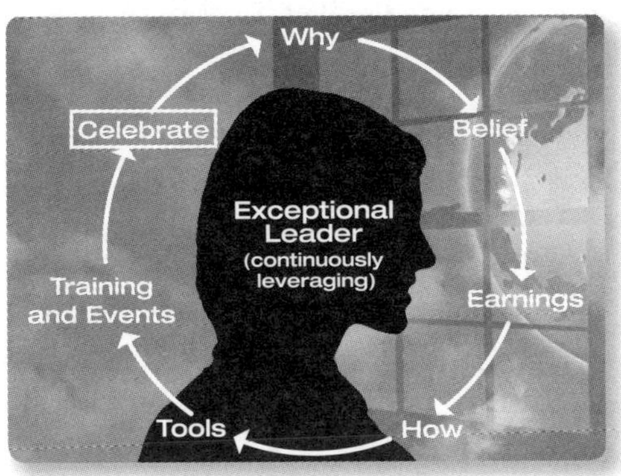

Step 7 – Celebrate

Great leaders create memorable moments

I share with my leaders at every opportunity how important it is to enjoy the business. We celebrate every accomplishment no matter how small. We believe in our abilities to be among Avon's best. We keep working with the good to help them become great and the great to become excellent and to always remember that we chose to embrace network marketing because we sincerely believe that this industry changes lives. We also chose this industry because we don't want to live on minimum or average earnings; we want to earn an income equal to our personal ambition. We understand now that to maximize our opportunity we must create plans and follow them—consistently.

I have now taken you through my complete cycle of success. It has worked for me, and it is working for 100s of Representatives in my dynamic downline. Because of the success that I have personally experienced and because of the incredible successes my downline members are experiencing, I am convinced that the cycle will work for you, too. The difference between success and failure is the resolve to stick to your plan long enough to win. I encourage all of you to plan to win!

As I close the story of my journey to Senior Executive Unit Leader in 20 months, I encourage you to take another look at the ***Accelerated Success Cycle©***. It worked for me and my downline and it will work for you. You can jump into the cycle at any point, based on what's going on in your life; the important thing is to jump in and take the appropriate steps to move your business forward. You can become an Exceptional Leader faster than you think.

When I am working with my downline, I like to start the cycle at the **"why"** so that I can make a true connection with my new business partners early. I can then customize their success plan because each person embraces the opportunity for a different reason. I always document and ask leading questions and sometimes I have to help them identify their "why."

Remember, I joined Avon because I wanted to earn $100 extra every month, but then six months later my "why" changed, and my business plan did as well; that is why it is very important to revisit your "why" and those of your downline often.

My **"Belief"** point on the cycle changed when I watched the *Avon's Rich and Famous* and *Women in the Spotlight* DVDs. And my belief was strengthened when my upline, Peter and Bernadett Calamaras, reassured me that I could achieve success and provide for my family. What Peter and Bernadette did that impacted my business the most was they taught me how to become a strategic thinker. They called me everyday to review my progress, to discuss short and long term goals and to make sure I stayed focused. In fact, the 20 Accelerated Success Actions listed on page 64 was greatly influenced by the activities they encouraged me to do daily. Now I do the same for my downline members today. Make sure your belief is consistent with your dreams and goals.

The **"Earnings"** became my focus after Peter, my upline, instilled confidence in me by explaining that I could earn serious money with Avon. He took the time to help me develop a specific plan to work my business to achieve President's Club and Senior Executive Unit Leader status like he had. That was all the motivation I needed to begin working my business everyday. I am proud to share that my earnings continue to grow, even today. I also encourage my downline members to take advantage of every opportunity to earn Avon's money. We work hard as a team to earn at the highest levels every two weeks. We plan at every opportunity to not leave any incentive or bonus money on Avon's table!

I made it my responsibility to learn **"how"** to become a stronger leader. I attend every training event Avon provides; I read about successful leaders both inside and outside of Avon. I often ask my top leaders questions about how I could be better at supporting them. And if they ask me to provide something that I didn't know how to provide, I make an effort to find the answers for them.

I embrace all of Avon's **"business development tools,"** and I have stopped creating things in my office. I only use what Avon provides because I want my leaders to be able to provide the same support to their downlines as I am providing to them. I have fallen in love with the Downline Manager Genealogy tool and the Beauty of Knowledge—not to mention all of the other tools Avon provides to help each of us achieve success from our homes. We try our best to maximize everything, such as the Fast Start Bonus, Mentor Bonus, and President's Club awards, just to name a few. Our goal is to use every tool possible to help our new recruits earn Unit Leader status within their first two to three months.

"Training and Events": I now focus more on my new Representatives; I create my calendar around my new recruits' needs, making sure they receive all the support they need to launch a successful business in their first 90 days.

And believe me, I wasn't very strong with my follow-up two years ago.

"Celebrate": It's important to celebrate all successes both big and small along the way. We have a lot to celebrate, and I encourage each of you to celebrate every accomplishment; no matter how small, keep working with the good to help them become great and the great to become excellent. Always believe in your ability to be one of Avon's best. I encourage all of you to use this ***Accelerated Success Cycle***© and the attached calendar examples to create plans for yourself and your downline members. Winston Churchill said it best, "Never give up!"

Accelerated Success Cycle

Celebrate

- ✓ Instill confidence
- ✓ Have FUN!
- ✓ Recognize early achievements:
- ✓ Fast Start Bonus
- ✓ 4 consecutive orders
- ✓ Milestones…Etc.

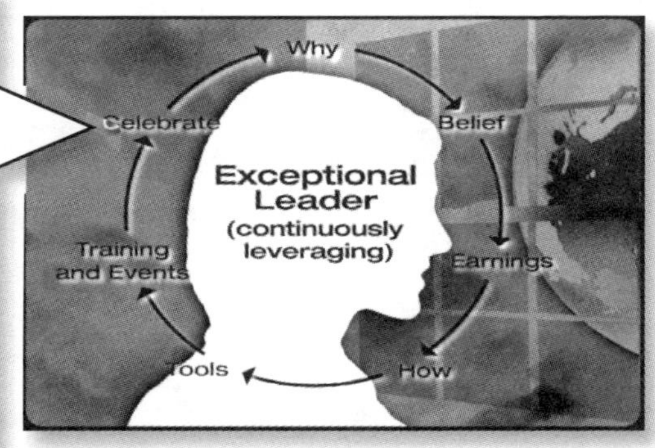

Thanks for reading my story… and I wish you accelerated success!

"Saddle your dreams before you ride 'em."

– Mary Webb

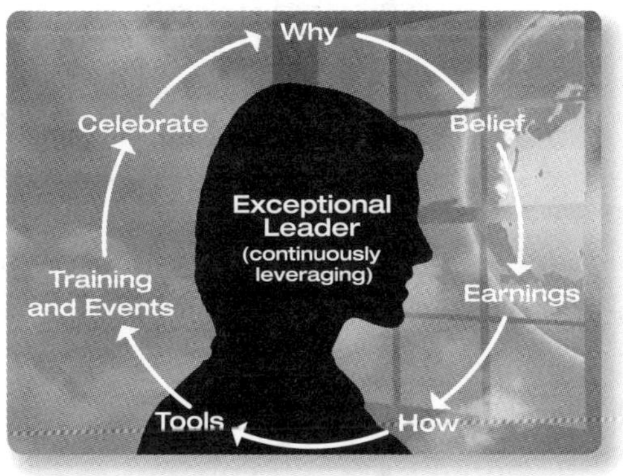

Accelerate Your Success

Tim Sales, a successful network marketing trainer and author of the *Brilliant Compensation*, series wrote a great article entitled, "Build MLM Part Time." He explains the three most important assets we must manage to be able to achieve success in this industry as ***money, time and attention.***

He suggests that we budget all three of these assets, carefully. The example he shares about money is that he decided while working full time in the navy that he would invest $400 per month to build his network marketing business. He actually created a budget to spend a $100 on buying tools, $250 went to running ads or on lead generation, and $50 was spent on buying books, tapes, and educational items so that he could personally gain more knowledge and become more effective.

Tim encourages us also to budget our time and attention. Here is a quick example of how he refocused his priorities around his time. He created a personal mantra that he used many times every day, which was, "I will only do activities that will contribute to my ability to earn $10,000* a month." When I first read this, I thought, No way…$10,000* a month from a part-time home business? Well, in less than two years my earnings from my home business consistently exceed $10,000* a month, too.

Reading this statement from Tim helped me determine my priorities, and it also helped me to stay focused on the important activities that contributed most to a successful network marketing business.

In addition, I found Tim's focus on managing what you must pay attention to on a daily basis even more empowering. Go to his website and read the entire article; the article is another example of how you can change how you see the world: www.brilliantcompensation.com

Once you take control of your three most important assets, it's time for you to plan ways to accelerate your personal actions to achieve your goals. Most of us rise in the morning at 6:00 a.m. and we end our days around 10:00 p.m. That's a total of 16 hours a day. You must ask yourself, "How many activities do I complete each day that directly impact the growth of my business? Or, how many of the 16 hours did I spend on achieving my dreams?" Amazingly, you can make great improvements in your life with an initial investment of two to three hours a day or 10 - 15 hours a week.

Start by determining a mission for each day of the week. For example, Monday could be your day to work with your top Unit Leaders, helping them advance their business units. Tuesday could be the day that you work your potential Unit Leaders, conducting 90-day business planning sessions for title advancement and so on, with a specific plan or mission for each day of the week.

---

* Your earnings may vary.

Take a look at the ***Accelerate Your Personal Actions Planner*** on page 64 and really think about the power of having 16 hours a day available to you to change your dreams and to be able to change your life. Moving forward, determine which of your 16 hours will be your ***"prime time"*** hours and protect those hours. If you choose your prime time to be between 7:00 p.m. and 9:00 p.m. because you work a full-time job or 10:00 a.m. - 12:00 noon after sending your children off to school, it's important that you make sure you focus your prime time on the "right" activities, strategies, and tasks consistently.

It's the same for television executives who program their best shows during the prime time hours of 7:00 - 9:00 p.m., and they charge advertisers the most to advertise during those peak times, because they know that's when most people are in front of the T.V. They do this to increase their profits, and if you want more out of your business, you must do the same. Start by asking yourself, "Which hours today did I earn the most, sell the most, or recruit the most customers or sellers to my business and why?"

What time of the day seems to work best for conducting uninterrupted business planning sessions with my strong leaders and why? Once you understand the "why" behind your actions, it will not take much for you to make a commitment to repeat those behaviors.

Focus on adding ***new business*** every day during ***prime time hours*** and commit to training and following up with your downline at other hours of the day. Once you have clarified your mission for each day, then review the list of activities and develop your strategies to make sure you pay attention to the amount of time you spend on each one. Consistency is the key to long-term earnings for both you and your downline. When you better manage your time, attention, and money as taught by Tim Sales, you will achieve your dreams.

Accelerate Your Personal Actions Planner (APAP)

Re-launch your business as a serious network marketer.

1. I know you use a planner; however, for the next 30 days work with the (APAP) planner concept, and then you can go back to your regular planner with a clear understanding of which activities you must focus on every day to achieve success.

2. We all have the same 16 hours every day. How you choose to spend your time will determine how soon you will achieve your goals. Start with a focus on two to three hours a day. As you learn to manage your time around the "right activities," you can make adjustments later to add a few more actions that will increase your effectiveness as a leader.

3. Next, determine what will be your daily business development mission. What will be the major priority for the day? Sure you will do other things, but what is the most important objective of each day of the week? Remember, every day you must complete activities that will get you closer to your goals. Adding structure and consistency is a critical component to your success.

4. Determine of the 16 hours you have daily which are your "prime time" hours. Select the hours that will

allow you the time to complete several of the activities listed on the APAP. For the next 30 days, protect and preserve the hours you have selected. Remember, you are developing a plan to change how you see the world so that you can change how you live in the world.

5. Review the list of 20 "accelerated" activities and determine how many you are currently doing daily, weekly, or monthly. Ask your upline or District Manager for clarity on any you may not understand, and based on how many you are currently using, accelerate your actions by selecting two or three more.

6. After you have created your week or campaign of activities using the APAP, at the end of each day place a check mark beside each activity you are able to complete that day. Exceptional leaders are able to complete 10 or more of the listed activities every day—consistently.

7. Consistency and self-discipline are critical to your success. Use the APAP for 30 days, and you will develop the behaviors of an exceptional leader. Once you have paid attention to the key actions that will improve your personal results, you will then be ready to select three of your high potential performers to teach them to do the same as you. You will then be poised to watch your earnings explode, as mine have!

1 Accelerate Your Personal Actions Planner (APAP)

2	Accelerated Personal Actions Planner	Day & Daily Mission 3
6: 00		
7:00		
8:00		
9:00		
10:00		5
11:00	4	**Accelerated Earnings Actions**
		Accelerated Coaching Activities with Downline
12:00	**Prime Time** are the hours of the day that you will commit to finding, **developing**, and **growing** your business.	Appointments & Interviews
		Seminar, Workshop, Retreat, Conference
1:00		Accelerated Business Planning
		Collect & Deliver Customer Orders
2:00		Conference Calls: Development & Recognition
		Downline Manager Reports & Planning
3:00		Generate New Orders/Face-to-face & Online
	6	Follow-ups: Leads/No or Low –Orders
4:00		Fundraising Presentations
		Listen to Skill Enhancing CDs
5:00		New Recruits Training Contacts
		Online Training Courses
6:00		Opportunity Presentations, Referrals
		Phone Dials for Referrals & Following Up
7:00	4	Prospecting/Power Hour
		Product Promotions/Open House Selling
8:00	**Prime Time** are the hours of the day that you will commit to finding, **developing**, and **growing** your business.	Reading Business Development Books
		Sales Meeting/Unit Meeting/Other Meeting
9:00		Top Performers Recognition
10:00		

7 **Consistency and self-discipline are the "keys" to your dreams!**

Accelerated Action Activities Chart

Exceptional leaders complete a minimum of 10 accelerated action activities everyday focusing more than 50% of their time on the activities that will impact the three "Ps (product, people and profits)."

# of Activities	Total Activities Listed	What % of the 20 Activities are you spending time on?
1	20	5%
2	20	10%
3	20	15%
4	20	20%
5	20	25%
6	20	30%
7	20	35%
8	20	40%
9	20	45%
10	20	50%
11	20	55%
12	20	60%
13	20	65%
14	20	70%
15	20	75%
16	20	80%
17	20	85%
18	20	90%
19	20	95%
20	20	100%

Paying attention to what you do is the difference between earning a little or a lot. If you completed six of the 20 activities listed in one day, congratulations! Your day was productive.

You were able to focus on 30% of the activities available to you to increase your earnings.

Each activity listed is a tested and proven method, task or strategy that will accelerate the growth of your business unit. What's more important is that the activities listed are the behaviors you must teach others to do consistently in your downline. Your business model must include as many of these activities as possible. To earn six-figures, you've got to figure out how to complete 10 or more of the activities listed every day—consistently.

To better illustrate the importance of this point, take a look (page 67) at how I spent my days when I worked full time in the beauty salon. I had no real focus and I didn't work my network marketing business consistently. My time was limited, and I struggled daily to get all of the things done on my to-do list for my family, the salon and my business.

Take a look (page 68) at how my days are planned now that I am able to work my business full time. I have a clear mission for each day, and I maximize my time by doing what I have to so that I am able to provide a bright future for my children.

As you can see from my current schedule by refocusing my time on more of the specific "accelerated earnings activities," I am now more productive and in control of my life and business. I have a clear mission for each day, and while Mondays are my longest work day of the week, I am able to spend more than 50% of the day on the right activities while still finding time for my family's priorities, which are preparing dinner, helping my kids with homework, and having family worship time.

Past Planner with No Real Focus

My Part-Time Network Marketing Schedule		Monday	
6: am	Dressed kids for school	A1	Call Doctor
	Pack lunches & snacks	A2	Grocery
7:00	Breakfast and get kids off to school	B1	Prepare Appointment Kits
	Review DLM report, returned calls	B2	Label books
8:00	Deliver Avon order, pass out brochures	C	Send ecards
	Drive to salon	B3	Calling Customers
9:00		A3	Calling Downline members
10:00	**Beauty Salon Job**		
11:00			
12:00	Appoint Alice		**Accelerated Earnings Actions**
	Deliver orders to shop customers		Accelerated Coaching Activities with Downline
1:00		√	Appointments & Interviews
			Seminar, Workshop, Retreat, Conference
2:00			Accelerated Business Planning
			Collect & Deliver Customer Orders
3:00	**Beauty Salon Job**		Conference Calls: Development & Recognition
		√	Downline Manager Reports & Planning
4:00		√	Generate New Orders/Face-to-face & Online
		√	Follow-ups: Leads/No or Low –Orders
5:00			Fundraising Presentations
			Listen to Skill Enhancing CDs
6:00	Drive home		New Recruits Training Contacts
	Prepare dinner		Online Training Courses
7:00	Eat dinner with family		Opportunity Presentations, Referrals
	Homework w Kids/Pack Kits		Phone Dials for Referrals & Following Up
8:00	Label brochures w Kids		Prospecting/Power Hour
	Put Kids to bed	√	Product Promotions/Open House Selling
9:00	Return calls & emails		Reading Business Development Books
			Sales Meeting/Unit Meeting/Other Meeting
10:00	Review Downline Reports		Top Performers Recognition

Accelerate Your Personal Actions Planner (APAP)

My Full-Time Network Marketing Schedule		Monday Developing Leaders Day	
6: 00	Rise, dress to work in home office	B	Order RF DVD
	Prepare & eat breakfast	B	Get Gas
7:00	Send kids off	A	Bank Deposit
	Check DLM reports for order count activities, send and check email	C	Call Sister
8:00	AUL Pasha conference call review group activities & fundraiser		
9:00	EUL Solomon & his AUL Debbie conference call to review and plan next 90-days		
10:00			
	EUL Michelle conf call , Tena, Tara/ To Strategizing on how to win PC incentive		
11:00			
12:00			**Accelerated Earnings Actions**
	AUL Tanesha call – plan $3000 open house	✓	Accelerated Coaching Activities with Downline
1:00		✓	Appointments & Interviews
	Lunch & Listen to Bob Proctor's CD: *Profits are Better Than Wages*		Seminar, Workshop, Retreat, Conference
2:00	90-Day Planning Session Call: Veronica – 2 new UL/Set goal for 1 new UL every month	✓	Accelerated Business Planning
		✓	Collect & Deliver Customer Orders
3:00		✓	Conference Calls: Development & Recognition
		✓	Downline Manager Reports & Planning
4:00			Generate New Orders/Face-to-face & Online
	Prepare Dinner/ Yordan arrives from school	✓	Follow-ups: Leads/No or Low –Orders
5:00	Dinner with Yordan Keisha & Rhiannon		Fundraising Presentations
	Homework	✓	Listen to Skill Enhancing CDs
6:00			New Recruits Training Contacts
	Bible study with kids		Online Training Courses
7:00	Bible study with kids		Opportunity Presentations, Referrals
	Bible study with kids		Phone Dials for Referrals & Following Up
8:00			Prospecting/Power Hour
		✓	Product Promotions/Open House Selling
9:00	EUL Rose training on DLM to improve her 1st generation retention/plan Oppt Meeting		Reading Business Development Books
	Check & place online orders		Sales Meeting/Unit Meeting/Other Meeting
10:00	Laundry	✓	Top Performers Recognition

Are you ready to change your dreams... so that you can change your life?

It's time to plan your accelerated success strategy to achieve Senior Executive Unit Leader by committing to the use of the ***Accelerated Success Cycle***© and Daily APAP planner pages. Don't settle for minimum earnings now that you have joined the network marketing industry. Let me be the first to offer you an opportunity to earn an income based on your ambition. The network marketing industry allows ordinary people like me and you to earn an extraordinary income simply by helping others.

No matter what business you choose in the network marketing industry, it is possible for you to accelerate your earnings when you help a minimum of 10 people become successful leaders every year. Just think about it for a minute: Even if you are new to the business, multiply the total sales of your entire business unit by 10. Is that an impressive number? Now double that number again. Now you are starting to see the power of the industry. Only a few people will see the power behind the numbers, but when you find one of those network marketing thinkers, you must be ready to mentor him or her to success in an accelerated fashion or he or she will move on to the next opportunity.

"As you travel through life,
your dreams will guide you,
determination will get you there,
and love will provide the greatest scenery of all."

– Michelle C. Ustaszeski

Accelerated Success Cycle© Checklist

To become a Senior Executive Unit Leader in two years or less, focus on the activities below and help 10 others do the same. There are two important strategies you must focus on to achieve Senior Executive Unit Leader in two years or less. The first strategy is to increase the number of Unit Leaders in your downline to 10 or more so that you can sort through them to find two or three that have lofty goals and dreams like you. This is 10 new Unit Leaders over and above the number you currently have. You need some fresh thinkers, individuals that are "hungry" for a change. You must seek out business partners who are willing to invest 10 – 15 hours every week in the development of their business. Once you find these individuals you must then commit to the second strategy.

The second strategy is that you must support, develop, and encourage your future leaders to strive for excellence. Evaluate and ensure that your own "Belief Window" supports your goals and values.

In addition to re-working your calendars to reflect what you have learned in this book about protecting your prime time and using more of the "accelerated" activities on a daily basis, you can use the ***Accelerated Success Cycle***© Checklist below to speed up the performance of your high potential and current leaders. Identify two or three downline members that you will work with using the ***Accelerated Success Cycle***© checklist on the following pages. Commit to using the cycle to help your leaders change their dreams about a brighter and better tomorrow.

Make a commitment to help a minimum of 10 people this year increase their personal income as one of your new business partners. You may have to offer the business to a hundred people to find the 10 who will be leaders. But those 10 could build a million dollar business for you or they could increase your business by a million dollars in a year. However you look at it… 10 is the magic number.

Use the ***Accelerated Success Cycle***© Checklist to build business relationships early in your mentoring process. The checklist will help you stay focused on the seven steps that will improve both your performance and the performance of those you lead. When you focus on helping others, you will expand your circle of influence and be on your way to reaching new heights.

Complete a checklist on your high potential Unit Leaders and track their progress as you take them through the ***Accelerated Success Cycle***©. You must take each of your key downline members through all seven steps to achieve success. Check off each point as you move through the cycle with them; you may not complete them in sequence, and that's fine. Just plan to discuss all seven points as soon and as often as you can with those that have serious dreams for a better life.

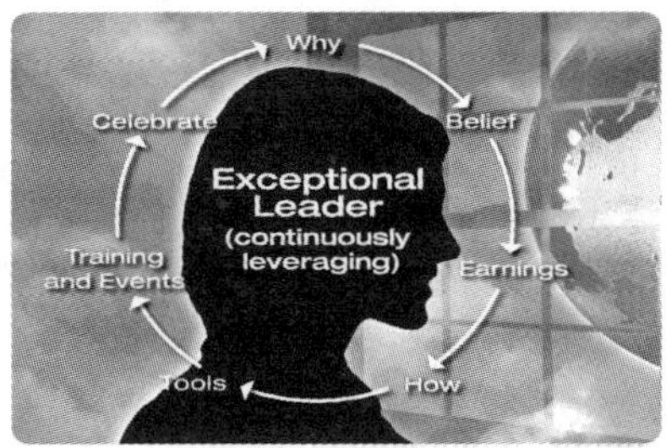

ACCELERATED SUCCESS CYCLE© CHECKLIST

Use this checklist to keep track of the business development discussions you have with your high potential leaders.

Downline member: ____________________

Titles: ____________________

Dream/Goals: ____________________

Starting date of discussion: ____________________

Date completed: ____________________

WHY: You must help your recruits clarify 'why' they want to do the business so that you can best lead and guide them to reach their goals and objectives.

- ❑ During the interview document why they are selecting the opportunity
- ❑ Use open-ended questions to get to the root of "why" they joined
- ❑ Discuss where they are today and clarify what they want to accomplish in six months to a year. Once the "why" is established, proceed to develop goals and dreams.

BELIEF: Understanding the power of what's on your "Belief Window" in relationship to your decisions will affect the speed of both your success and that of your downline

- ❑ Share good examples of how you changed your belief and then how you changed your results
- ❑ Encourage Representatives to identify their own beliefs and adjust their thinking to achieve success
- ❑ Share success stories and inspirational facts about the business
- ❑ Instill confidence in your downline by education and practice

EARNINGS: When explaining the earnings potential, always connect with ***"why"*** your Representative wants a home-based business. Share examples of the power of the earnings per hour potential, for example, "When I sell a $52 skin care cream, I earn $26 on a sale; that takes less than 30 minutes."

- ❑ Help your recruits earn the Fast Start bonus. Take them out prospecting and recruiting until they find their first five recruits. Then talk to them every other day until they find a minimum of 12 recruits to earn the total Fast Start bonus award
- ❑ Focus on helping your new recruits maximize their earning opportunity in the first two months so that they can continue to earn at the highest level
- ❑ Link the Fast Start bonus opportunity to becoming a Unit Leader in two months and an Advanced Unit Leader in six months
- ❑ Establish timeframes and goals to receive Leadership check within three months

HOW: Create visions of success for your high potential leaders. Develop your plans in 30, 60 and 90-day time blocks to allow for balance of both business (sell, share & show) and personal priorities. Include 8 to 10 of the accelerated actions everyday.

- ❑ Prospect daily, generate leads, set goals for number of new customers and Recruits for every campaign
- ❑ Appoint a minimum of two to three new recruits every week
  - ❍ Follow Appointment/signup process
  - ❍ Develop a contact list of 100-plus face-to-face, telephone and Internet contacts
  - ❍ Teach how to get $25 orders from 20 Customers each campaign
- ❑ Train only on the tools that are easily available to your downline.

TOOLS: Explain the tools in an easy-to-understand way to ensure duplication.

- ❑ Prospecting Tools:
  - ❍ Prospecting Flyers/Business Cards/DVD/CDs
  - ❍ Opportunity Presentations/Success Hours
  - ❍ Distribute 100- 200 brochures per campaign with Prospecting Flyers/ DVDs
- ❑ Downline Manager Tools and Web Office resources
- ❑ Accelerated/90-Day Business Planning Sessions

TRAINING AND EVENTS: Include one-on-one nourishment, weekly phone contacts, group training, workshops, and online training with your downline.

- ❑ New Representative Training Contacts on Selling and Sharing
- ❑ Online Training
  - ❍ Online training courses for skill enhancements
  - ❍ Networking Marketing Online Courses
  - ❍ Looking for Leaders network marketing workshop
- ❑ Observing upline/downline as they prospect, recruit and train others
- ❑ Use the company's training materials to increase retention and sales
- ❑ Conference calls are a great way to train and inspire a small group of downline members on key "accelerated action" topics
- ❑ Teach downline the skills of selling and sharing the opportunity

CELEBRATE: Celebrate, reward, and recognize successes both large and small. Look for short-term wins and make them big milestones in the minds of your downline members.

- ❑ Instill confidence in your leaders with recognition
- ❑ Have fun everyday helping someone discover their strengths
- ❑ Recognize early achievements, for example:

- 10 new Customers
- First $500 in total sales
- Earning the Fast Start bonus
- First recruit
- Distribute first 100 brochures
- Earned Unit Leader pins
- First short-term goal achieved
- Four consecutive orders
- First Fundraiser
- First male customer
- First office building with customers
- Distributed 10 Prospecting DVDs/Flyers
- First open house
- Completed all online courses
- First 5 customer orders over $25
- First customer with $100 order

Minor and Major Accomplishments to Recognize & Honor:

____

____

____

"Work harder on yourself
than you do at a job.
When you work at your job,
you make a living.
When you work on yourself,
you'll make a fortune."

– Jim Rohn

Dream Changers Who Changed

"My dreams when I started Avon were to be an independent provider for my family. Being a single mother, I could hardly make ends meet. My major goal was to be able to provide for my family in the best way possible. My goal now is to become a homeowner. Since I am living my dream, which is to provide for my family, I want to make a bigger step—to purchase a home for my children so that we can enjoy life and feel secure knowing that we have a home of our own. I will never forget where I started, and I will always be grateful for all of the support you have given me because those memories are my road map to success. Marcus M. Garvey once said that 'A people without the knowledge of their past history, origin and culture is like a tree without roots.'"

Claudette Walter
Avon *Executive Unit Leader & President's Club Member*

"I want to tell you that our telephone talk has motivated me and has given me the confidence that I needed. I am quitting the Beauty Shop at the end of January to devote myself to my Avon business, and I expect to have over a million dollar business in 2008 as a Senior Executive Unit Leader. I have been waiting until now to tell you that if everyone puts in and pays for their campaign 25 orders, I will be an Executive Unit Leader. I have new people that have seen the dream and are working harder. Coleen Bedair signed her sixth person tonight. Rebecca Ramos has six, and Gay Kelley has five recruits, along with my three steady Unit Leaders. I am also working with Victoria Day's first generation that rolled up, which will count toward my numbers in campaign four as my seventh Unit Leader. I have three or four more 1st generations working and five or six, 2nd and 3rd generations on track, too. Until we spoke I didn't really believe that this would ever happen. Thank you for helping me believe. From the bottom of my heart, thank you."

Benna Resnick from Dallas, Texas,
Executive Unit Leader & Honor Society Member

Accelerate Your Personal Success

"Do what you have to do so that you can do what you want to do a year from now…"

I am changing my dreams from page 13.

To much *Bigger*, life-changing goals….

30 – Days from now… **By Date: ________**

60 – Days from now… **By Date: ________**

90 – Days from now… **By Date: ________**

A year from now… **By Date: ________**

APPENDIX

Accelerate Your Personal Actions Planner Pages (APAP)

Determine where you want your business to be in the next 30-days and then use the following pages to select your prime time hours. Remember, your days can vary based on your personal and business commitments. Keep track of the activities you are able to complete each day. And set your goal to be completing 8 to 10 activities a day by the end of the 30-day period.

Send me an e:mail on your accelerated results!

accelerated success.reidmitchel@gmail.com

ACCELERATE YOUR PERSONAL ACTIONS PLANNER (APAP)

My Schedule with (APAPs)		Day/Date: Mission:	
6:00 am			
7:00 am			
8:00 am			
9:00 am			
10:00 am			
11:00 am			
12:00 pm			**Accelerated Earnings Actions**
			Accelerated Coaching Activities with Downline
1:00 pm			Appointments & Interviews
			Accelerated Business Planning
2:00 pm			Collect & Deliver Customer Orders
			Conference Calls: Development & Recognition
3:00 pm			Downline Manager Reports & Planning
			Generate New Orders/Face-to-face & Online
4:00 pm			Follow-ups: Leads/No or Low –Orders
			Fundraising Presentations
5:00 pm			Listen to Skill Enhancing CDs
			New Recruits Training Contacts
6:00 pm			Online Training Courses
			Opportunity Presentations, Referrals
7:00 pm			Phone Dials for Referrals & Following Up
			Prospecting/Power Hour
8:00 pm			Product Promotions/Open House Selling
			Reading Business Development Books
9:00 pm			Sales Meeting/Unit Meeting/Other Meeting
			Seminar, Workshop, Retreat, Conference
10:00 pm			Top Performers Recognition

ACCELERATE YOUR PERSONAL ACTIONS PLANNER (APAP)

My Schedule with (APAPs)		Day/Date: Mission:	
6:00 am			
7:00 am			
8:00 am			
9:00 am			
10:00 am			
11:00 am			
12:00 pm			**Accelerated Earnings Actions**
			Accelerated Coaching Activities with Downline
1:00 pm			Appointments & Interviews
			Accelerated Business Planning
2:00 pm			Collect & Deliver Customer Orders
			Conference Calls: Development & Recognition
3:00 pm			Downline Manager Reports & Planning
			Generate New Orders/Face-to-face & Online
4:00 pm			Follow-ups: Leads/No or Low –Orders
			Fundraising Presentations
5:00 pm			Listen to Skill Enhancing CDs
			New Recruits Training Contacts
6:00 pm			Online Training Courses
			Opportunity Presentations, Referrals
7:00 pm			Phone Dials for Referrals & Following Up
			Prospecting/Power Hour
8:00 pm			Product Promotions/Open House Selling
			Reading Business Development Books
9:00 pm			Sales Meeting/Unit Meeting/Other Meeting
			Seminar, Workshop, Retreat, Conference
10:00 pm			Top Performers Recognition

Accelerate your Personal Actions Planner (APAP)

My Schedule with (APAPs)		Day/Date: Mission:	
6:00 am			
7:00 am			
8:00 am			
9:00 am			
10:00 am			
11:00 am			
12:00 pm			**Accelerated Earnings Actions**
			Accelerated Coaching Activities with Downline
1:00 pm			Appointments & Interviews
			Accelerated Business Planning
2:00 pm			Collect & Deliver Customer Orders
			Conference Calls: Development & Recognition
3:00 pm			Downline Manager Reports & Planning
			Generate New Orders/Face-to-face & Online
4:00 pm			Follow-ups: Leads/No or Low –Orders
			Fundraising Presentations
5:00 pm			Listen to Skill Enhancing CDs
			New Recruits Training Contacts
6:00 pm			Online Training Courses
			Opportunity Presentations, Referrals
7:00 pm			Phone Dials for Referrals & Following Up
			Prospecting/Power Hour
8:00 pm			Product Promotions/Open House Selling
			Reading Business Development Books
9:00 pm			Sales Meeting/Unit Meeting/Other Meeting
			Seminar, Workshop, Retreat, Conference
10:00 pm			Top Performers Recognition

Accelerate your Personal Actions Planner (APAP)

My Schedule with (APAPs)		Day/Date:	
		Mission:	
6:00 am			
7:00 am			
8:00 am			
9:00 am			
10:00 am			
11:00 am			
12:00 pm			**Accelerated Earnings Actions**
			Accelerated Coaching Activities with Downline
1:00 pm			Appointments & Interviews
			Accelerated Business Planning
2:00 pm			Collect & Deliver Customer Orders
			Conference Calls: Development & Recognition
3:00 pm			Downline Manager Reports & Planning
			Generate New Orders/Face-to-face & Online
4:00 pm			Follow-ups: Leads/No or Low –Orders
			Fundraising Presentations
5:00 pm			Listen to Skill Enhancing CDs
			New Recruits Training Contacts
6:00 pm			Online Training Courses
			Opportunity Presentations, Referrals
7:00 pm			Phone Dials for Referrals & Following Up
			Prospecting/Power Hour
8:00 pm			Product Promotions/Open House Selling
			Reading Business Development Books
9:00 pm			Sales Meeting/Unit Meeting/Other Meeting
			Seminar, Workshop, Retreat, Conference
10:00 pm			Top Performers Recognition

ACCELERATE YOUR PERSONAL ACTIONS PLANNER (APAP)

My Schedule with (APAPs)		**Day/Date:** **Mission:**	
6:00 am			
7:00 am			
8:00 am			
9:00 am			
10:00 am			
11:00 am			
12:00 pm			**Accelerated Earnings Actions**
			Accelerated Coaching Activities with Downline
1:00 pm			Appointments & Interviews
			Accelerated Business Planning
2:00 pm			Collect & Deliver Customer Orders
			Conference Calls: Development & Recognition
3:00 pm			Downline Manager Reports & Planning
			Generate New Orders/Face-to-face & Online
4:00 pm			Follow-ups: Leads/No or Low –Orders
			Fundraising Presentations
5:00 pm			Listen to Skill Enhancing CDs
			New Recruits Training Contacts
6:00 pm			Online Training Courses
			Opportunity Presentations, Referrals
7:00 pm			Phone Dials for Referrals & Following Up
			Prospecting/Power Hour
8:00 pm			Product Promotions/Open House Selling
			Reading Business Development Books
9:00 pm			Sales Meeting/Unit Meeting/Other Meeting
			Seminar, Workshop, Retreat, Conference
10:00 pm			Top Performers Recognition

Accelerate your Personal Actions Planner (APAP)

My Schedule with (APAPs)		Day/Date: Mission:	
6:00 am			
7:00 am			
8:00 am			
9:00 am			
10:00 am			
11:00 am			
12:00 pm			**Accelerated Earnings Actions**
			Accelerated Coaching Activities with Downline
1:00 pm			Appointments & Interviews
			Accelerated Business Planning
2:00 pm			Collect & Deliver Customer Orders
			Conference Calls: Development & Recognition
3:00 pm			Downline Manager Reports & Planning
			Generate New Orders/Face-to-face & Online
4:00 pm			Follow-ups: Leads/No or Low –Orders
			Fundraising Presentations
5:00 pm			Listen to Skill Enhancing CDs
			New Recruits Training Contacts
6:00 pm			Online Training Courses
			Opportunity Presentations, Referrals
7:00 pm			Phone Dials for Referrals & Following Up
			Prospecting/Power Hour
8:00 pm			Product Promotions/Open House Selling
			Reading Business Development Books
9:00 pm			Sales Meeting/Unit Meeting/Other Meeting
			Seminar, Workshop, Retreat, Conference
10:00 pm			Top Performers Recognition

Accelerate your Personal Actions Planner (APAP)

My Schedule with (APAPs)		Day/Date: Mission:	
6:00 am			
7:00 am			
8:00 am			
9:00 am			
10:00 am			
11:00 am			
12:00 pm			**Accelerated Earnings Actions**
			Accelerated Coaching Activities with Downline
1:00 pm			Appointments & Interviews
			Accelerated Business Planning
2:00 pm			Collect & Deliver Customer Orders
			Conference Calls: Development & Recognition
3:00 pm			Downline Manager Reports & Planning
			Generate New Orders/Face-to-face & Online
4:00 pm			Follow-ups: Leads/No or Low –Orders
			Fundraising Presentations
5:00 pm			Listen to Skill Enhancing CDs
			New Recruits Training Contacts
6:00 pm			Online Training Courses
			Opportunity Presentations, Referrals
7:00 pm			Phone Dials for Referrals & Following Up
			Prospecting/Power Hour
8:00 pm			Product Promotions/Open House Selling
			Reading Business Development Books
9:00 pm			Sales Meeting/Unit Meeting/Other Meeting
			Seminar, Workshop, Retreat, Conference
10:00 pm			Top Performers Recognition

Accelerate your Personal Actions Planner (APAP)

My Schedule with (APAPs)		Day/Date: Mission:	
6:00 am			
7:00 am			
8:00 am			
9:00 am			
10:00 am			
11:00 am			
12:00 pm			**Accelerated Earnings Actions**
			Accelerated Coaching Activities with Downline
1:00 pm			Appointments & Interviews
			Accelerated Business Planning
2:00 pm			Collect & Deliver Customer Orders
			Conference Calls: Development & Recognition
3:00 pm			Downline Manager Reports & Planning
			Generate New Orders/Face-to-face & Online
4:00 pm			Follow-ups: Leads/No or Low –Orders
			Fundraising Presentations
5:00 pm			Listen to Skill Enhancing CDs
			New Recruits Training Contacts
6:00 pm			Online Training Courses
			Opportunity Presentations, Referrals
7:00 pm			Phone Dials for Referrals & Following Up
			Prospecting/Power Hour
8:00 pm			Product Promotions/Open House Selling
			Reading Business Development Books
9:00 pm			Sales Meeting/Unit Meeting/Other Meeting
			Seminar, Workshop, Retreat, Conference
10:00 pm			Top Performers Recognition

ACCELERATE YOUR PERSONAL ACTIONS PLANNER (APAP)

My Schedule with (APAPs)		Day/Date: Mission:	
6:00 am			
7:00 am			
8:00 am			
9:00 am			
10:00 am			
11:00 am			
12:00 pm			**Accelerated Earnings Actions**
			Accelerated Coaching Activities with Downline
1:00 pm			Appointments & Interviews
			Accelerated Business Planning
2:00 pm			Collect & Deliver Customer Orders
			Conference Calls: Development & Recognition
3:00 pm			Downline Manager Reports & Planning
			Generate New Orders/Face-to-face & Online
4:00 pm			Follow-ups: Leads/No or Low –Orders
			Fundraising Presentations
5:00 pm			Listen to Skill Enhancing CDs
			New Recruits Training Contacts
6:00 pm			Online Training Courses
			Opportunity Presentations, Referrals
7:00 pm			Phone Dials for Referrals & Following Up
			Prospecting/Power Hour
8:00 pm			Product Promotions/Open House Selling
			Reading Business Development Books
9:00 pm			Sales Meeting/Unit Meeting/Other Meeting
			Seminar, Workshop, Retreat, Conference
10:00 pm			Top Performers Recognition

ACCELERATE YOUR PERSONAL ACTIONS PLANNER (APAP)

My Schedule with (APAPs)		**Day/Date:** **Mission:**	
6:00 am			
7:00 am			
8:00 am			
9:00 am			
10:00 am			
11:00 am			
12:00 pm			**Accelerated Earnings Actions**
			Accelerated Coaching Activities with Downline
1:00 pm			Appointments & Interviews
			Accelerated Business Planning
2:00 pm			Collect & Deliver Customer Orders
			Conference Calls: Development & Recognition
3:00 pm			Downline Manager Reports & Planning
			Generate New Orders/Face-to-face & Online
4:00 pm			Follow-ups: Leads/No or Low –Orders
			Fundraising Presentations
5:00 pm			Listen to Skill Enhancing CDs
			New Recruits Training Contacts
6:00 pm			Online Training Courses
			Opportunity Presentations, Referrals
7:00 pm			Phone Dials for Referrals & Following Up
			Prospecting/Power Hour
8:00 pm			Product Promotions/Open House Selling
			Reading Business Development Books
9:00 pm			Sales Meeting/Unit Meeting/Other Meeting
			Seminar, Workshop, Retreat, Conference
10:00 pm			Top Performers Recognition

ACCELERATE YOUR PERSONAL ACTIONS PLANNER (APAP)

My Schedule with (APAPs)		Day/Date: Mission:	
6:00 am			
7:00 am			
8:00 am			
9:00 am			
10:00 am			
11:00 am			
12:00 pm			**Accelerated Earnings Actions**
			Accelerated Coaching Activities with Downline
1:00 pm			Appointments & Interviews
			Accelerated Business Planning
2:00 pm			Collect & Deliver Customer Orders
			Conference Calls: Development & Recognition
3:00 pm			Downline Manager Reports & Planning
			Generate New Orders/Face-to-face & Online
4:00 pm			Follow-ups: Leads/No or Low –Orders
			Fundraising Presentations
5:00 pm			Listen to Skill Enhancing CDs
			New Recruits Training Contacts
6:00 pm			Online Training Courses
			Opportunity Presentations, Referrals
7:00 pm			Phone Dials for Referrals & Following Up
			Prospecting/Power Hour
8:00 pm			Product Promotions/Open House Selling
			Reading Business Development Books
9:00 pm			Sales Meeting/Unit Meeting/Other Meeting
			Seminar, Workshop, Retreat, Conference
10:00 pm			Top Performers Recognition

Accelerate your Personal Actions Planner (APAP)

My Schedule with (APAPs)		**Day/Date:** **Mission:**	
6:00 am			
7:00 am			
8:00 am			
9:00 am			
10:00 am			
11:00 am			
12:00 pm			**Accelerated Earnings Actions**
			Accelerated Coaching Activities with Downline
1:00 pm			Appointments & Interviews
			Accelerated Business Planning
2:00 pm			Collect & Deliver Customer Orders
			Conference Calls: Development & Recognition
3:00 pm			Downline Manager Reports & Planning
			Generate New Orders/Face-to-face & Online
4:00 pm			Follow-ups: Leads/No or Low –Orders
			Fundraising Presentations
5:00 pm			Listen to Skill Enhancing CDs
			New Recruits Training Contacts
6:00 pm			Online Training Courses
			Opportunity Presentations, Referrals
7:00 pm			Phone Dials for Referrals & Following Up
			Prospecting/Power Hour
8:00 pm			Product Promotions/Open House Selling
			Reading Business Development Books
9:00 pm			Sales Meeting/Unit Meeting/Other Meeting
			Seminar, Workshop, Retreat, Conference
10:00 pm			Top Performers Recognition

Accelerate your Personal Actions Planner (APAP)

My Schedule with (APAPs)		Day/Date: Mission:	
6:00 am			
7:00 am			
8:00 am			
9:00 am			
10:00 am			
11:00 am			
12:00 pm			**Accelerated Earnings Actions**
			Accelerated Coaching Activities with Downline
1:00 pm			Appointments & Interviews
			Accelerated Business Planning
2:00 pm			Collect & Deliver Customer Orders
			Conference Calls: Development & Recognition
3:00 pm			Downline Manager Reports & Planning
			Generate New Orders/Face-to-face & Online
4:00 pm			Follow-ups: Leads/No or Low –Orders
			Fundraising Presentations
5:00 pm			Listen to Skill Enhancing CDs
			New Recruits Training Contacts
6:00 pm			Online Training Courses
			Opportunity Presentations, Referrals
7:00 pm			Phone Dials for Referrals & Following Up
			Prospecting/Power Hour
8:00 pm			Product Promotions/Open House Selling
			Reading Business Development Books
9:00 pm			Sales Meeting/Unit Meeting/Other Meeting
			Seminar, Workshop, Retreat, Conference
10:00 pm			Top Performers Recognition

Accelerate your Personal Actions Planner (APAP)

My Schedule with (APAPs)		Day/Date: Mission:	
6:00 am			
7:00 am			
8:00 am			
9:00 am			
10:00 am			
11:00 am			
12:00 pm			**Accelerated Earnings Actions**
			Accelerated Coaching Activities with Downline
1:00 pm			Appointments & Interviews
			Accelerated Business Planning
2:00 pm			Collect & Deliver Customer Orders
			Conference Calls: Development & Recognition
3:00 pm			Downline Manager Reports & Planning
			Generate New Orders/Face-to-face & Online
4:00 pm			Follow-ups: Leads/No or Low –Orders
			Fundraising Presentations
5:00 pm			Listen to Skill Enhancing CDs
			New Recruits Training Contacts
6:00 pm			Online Training Courses
			Opportunity Presentations, Referrals
7:00 pm			Phone Dials for Referrals & Following Up
			Prospecting/Power Hour
8:00 pm			Product Promotions/Open House Selling
			Reading Business Development Books
9:00 pm			Sales Meeting/Unit Meeting/Other Meeting
			Seminar, Workshop, Retreat, Conference
10:00 pm			Top Performers Recognition

ACCELERATE YOUR PERSONAL ACTIONS PLANNER (APAP)

My Schedule with (APAPs)			Day/Date: Mission:
6:00 am			
7:00 am			
8:00 am			
9:00 am			
10:00 am			
11:00 am			
12:00 pm			**Accelerated Earnings Actions**
			Accelerated Coaching Activities with Downline
1:00 pm			Appointments & Interviews
			Accelerated Business Planning
2:00 pm			Collect & Deliver Customer Orders
			Conference Calls: Development & Recognition
3:00 pm			Downline Manager Reports & Planning
			Generate New Orders/Face-to-face & Online
4:00 pm			Follow-ups: Leads/No or Low –Orders
			Fundraising Presentations
5:00 pm			Listen to Skill Enhancing CDs
			New Recruits Training Contacts
6:00 pm			Online Training Courses
			Opportunity Presentations, Referrals
7:00 pm			Phone Dials for Referrals & Following Up
			Prospecting/Power Hour
8:00 pm			Product Promotions/Open House Selling
			Reading Business Development Books
9:00 pm			Sales Meeting/Unit Meeting/Other Meeting
			Seminar, Workshop, Retreat, Conference
10:00 pm			Top Performers Recognition

ACCELERATE YOUR PERSONAL ACTIONS PLANNER (APAP)

My Schedule with (APAPs)		Day/Date: Mission:	
6:00 am			
7:00 am			
8:00 am			
9:00 am			
10:00 am			
11:00 am			
12:00 pm			**Accelerated Earnings Actions**
			Accelerated Coaching Activities with Downline
1:00 pm			Appointments & Interviews
			Accelerated Business Planning
2:00 pm			Collect & Deliver Customer Orders
			Conference Calls: Development & Recognition
3:00 pm			Downline Manager Reports & Planning
			Generate New Orders/Face-to-face & Online
4:00 pm			Follow-ups: Leads/No or Low –Orders
			Fundraising Presentations
5:00 pm			Listen to Skill Enhancing CDs
			New Recruits Training Contacts
6:00 pm			Online Training Courses
			Opportunity Presentations, Referrals
7:00 pm			Phone Dials for Referrals & Following Up
			Prospecting/Power Hour
8:00 pm			Product Promotions/Open House Selling
			Reading Business Development Books
9:00 pm			Sales Meeting/Unit Meeting/Other Meeting
			Seminar, Workshop, Retreat, Conference
10:00 pm			Top Performers Recognition

Accelerate your Personal Actions Planner (APAP)

My Schedule with (APAPs)		**Day/Date:** **Mission:**	
6:00 am			
7:00 am			
8:00 am			
9:00 am			
10:00 am			
11:00 am			
12:00 pm			**Accelerated Earnings Actions**
			Accelerated Coaching Activities with Downline
1:00 pm			Appointments & Interviews
			Accelerated Business Planning
2:00 pm			Collect & Deliver Customer Orders
			Conference Calls: Development & Recognition
3:00 pm			Downline Manager Reports & Planning
			Generate New Orders/Face-to-face & Online
4:00 pm			Follow-ups: Leads/No or Low –Orders
			Fundraising Presentations
5:00 pm			Listen to Skill Enhancing CDs
			New Recruits Training Contacts
6:00 pm			Online Training Courses
			Opportunity Presentations, Referrals
7:00 pm			Phone Dials for Referrals & Following Up
			Prospecting/Power Hour
8:00 pm			Product Promotions/Open House Selling
			Reading Business Development Books
9:00 pm			Sales Meeting/Unit Meeting/Other Meeting
			Seminar, Workshop, Retreat, Conference
10:00 pm			Top Performers Recognition

Accelerate your Personal Actions Planner (APAP)

My Schedule with (APAPs)		**Day/Date:** **Mission:**	
6:00 am			
7:00 am			
8:00 am			
9:00 am			
10:00 am			
11:00 am			
12:00 pm			**Accelerated Earnings Actions**
			Accelerated Coaching Activities with Downline
1:00 pm			Appointments & Interviews
			Accelerated Business Planning
2:00 pm			Collect & Deliver Customer Orders
			Conference Calls: Development & Recognition
3:00 pm			Downline Manager Reports & Planning
			Generate New Orders/Face-to-face & Online
4:00 pm			Follow-ups: Leads/No or Low –Orders
			Fundraising Presentations
5:00 pm			Listen to Skill Enhancing CDs
			New Recruits Training Contacts
6:00 pm			Online Training Courses
			Opportunity Presentations, Referrals
7:00 pm			Phone Dials for Referrals & Following Up
			Prospecting/Power Hour
8:00 pm			Product Promotions/Open House Selling
			Reading Business Development Books
9:00 pm			Sales Meeting/Unit Meeting/Other Meeting
			Seminar, Workshop, Retreat, Conference
10:00 pm			Top Performers Recognition

Accelerate your Personal Actions Planner (APAP)

My Schedule with (APAPs)		Day/Date: Mission:	
6:00 am			
7:00 am			
8:00 am			
9:00 am			
10:00 am			
11:00 am			
12:00 pm			**Accelerated Earnings Actions**
			Accelerated Coaching Activities with Downline
1:00 pm			Appointments & Interviews
			Accelerated Business Planning
2:00 pm			Collect & Deliver Customer Orders
			Conference Calls: Development & Recognition
3:00 pm			Downline Manager Reports & Planning
			Generate New Orders/Face-to-face & Online
4:00 pm			Follow-ups: Leads/No or Low –Orders
			Fundraising Presentations
5:00 pm			Listen to Skill Enhancing CDs
			New Recruits Training Contacts
6:00 pm			Online Training Courses
			Opportunity Presentations, Referrals
7:00 pm			Phone Dials for Referrals & Following Up
			Prospecting/Power Hour
8:00 pm			Product Promotions/Open House Selling
			Reading Business Development Books
9:00 pm			Sales Meeting/Unit Meeting/Other Meeting
			Seminar, Workshop, Retreat, Conference
10:00 pm			Top Performers Recognition

Accelerate your Personal Actions Planner (APAP)

My Schedule with (APAPs)		Day/Date: Mission:	
6:00 am			
7:00 am			
8:00 am			
9:00 am			
10:00 am			
11:00 am			
12:00 pm			**Accelerated Earnings Actions**
			Accelerated Coaching Activities with Downline
1:00 pm			Appointments & Interviews
			Accelerated Business Planning
2:00 pm			Collect & Deliver Customer Orders
			Conference Calls: Development & Recognition
3:00 pm			Downline Manager Reports & Planning
			Generate New Orders/Face-to-face & Online
4:00 pm			Follow-ups: Leads/No or Low –Orders
			Fundraising Presentations
5:00 pm			Listen to Skill Enhancing CDs
			New Recruits Training Contacts
6:00 pm			Online Training Courses
			Opportunity Presentations, Referrals
7:00 pm			Phone Dials for Referrals & Following Up
			Prospecting/Power Hour
8:00 pm			Product Promotions/Open House Selling
			Reading Business Development Books
9:00 pm			Sales Meeting/Unit Meeting/Other Meeting
			Seminar, Workshop, Retreat, Conference
10:00 pm			Top Performers Recognition

Accelerate your Personal Actions Planner (APAP)

My Schedule with (APAPs)		Day/Date: Mission:	
6:00 am			
7:00 am			
8:00 am			
9:00 am			
10:00 am			
11:00 am			
12:00 pm			**Accelerated Earnings Actions**
			Accelerated Coaching Activities with Downline
1:00 pm			Appointments & Interviews
			Accelerated Business Planning
2:00 pm			Collect & Deliver Customer Orders
			Conference Calls: Development & Recognition
3:00 pm			Downline Manager Reports & Planning
			Generate New Orders/Face-to-face & Online
4:00 pm			Follow-ups: Leads/No or Low –Orders
			Fundraising Presentations
5:00 pm			Listen to Skill Enhancing CDs
			New Recruits Training Contacts
6:00 pm			Online Training Courses
			Opportunity Presentations, Referrals
7:00 pm			Phone Dials for Referrals & Following Up
			Prospecting/Power Hour
8:00 pm			Product Promotions/Open House Selling
			Reading Business Development Books
9:00 pm			Sales Meeting/Unit Meeting/Other Meeting
			Seminar, Workshop, Retreat, Conference
10:00 pm			Top Performers Recognition

ACCELERATE YOUR PERSONAL ACTIONS PLANNER (APAP)

My Schedule with (APAPs)		Day/Date: Mission:	
6:00 am			
7:00 am			
8:00 am			
9:00 am			
10:00 am			
11:00 am			
12:00 pm			**Accelerated Earnings Actions**
			Accelerated Coaching Activities with Downline
1:00 pm			Appointments & Interviews
			Accelerated Business Planning
2:00 pm			Collect & Deliver Customer Orders
			Conference Calls: Development & Recognition
3:00 pm			Downline Manager Reports & Planning
			Generate New Orders/Face-to-face & Online
4:00 pm			Follow-ups: Leads/No or Low –Orders
			Fundraising Presentations
5:00 pm			Listen to Skill Enhancing CDs
			New Recruits Training Contacts
6:00 pm			Online Training Courses
			Opportunity Presentations, Referrals
7:00 pm			Phone Dials for Referrals & Following Up
			Prospecting/Power Hour
8:00 pm			Product Promotions/Open House Selling
			Reading Business Development Books
9:00 pm			Sales Meeting/Unit Meeting/Other Meeting
			Seminar, Workshop, Retreat, Conference
10:00 pm			Top Performers Recognition

ACCELERATE YOUR PERSONAL ACTIONS PLANNER (APAP)

My Schedule with (APAPs)		Day/Date: Mission:	
6:00 am			
7:00 am			
8:00 am			
9:00 am			
10:00 am			
11:00 am			
12:00 pm			**Accelerated Earnings Actions**
			Accelerated Coaching Activities with Downline
1:00 pm			Appointments & Interviews
			Accelerated Business Planning
2:00 pm			Collect & Deliver Customer Orders
			Conference Calls: Development & Recognition
3:00 pm			Downline Manager Reports & Planning
			Generate New Orders/Face-to-face & Online
4:00 pm			Follow-ups: Leads/No or Low –Orders
			Fundraising Presentations
5:00 pm			Listen to Skill Enhancing CDs
			New Recruits Training Contacts
6:00 pm			Online Training Courses
			Opportunity Presentations, Referrals
7:00 pm			Phone Dials for Referrals & Following Up
			Prospecting/Power Hour
8:00 pm			Product Promotions/Open House Selling
			Reading Business Development Books
9:00 pm			Sales Meeting/Unit Meeting/Other Meeting
			Seminar, Workshop, Retreat, Conference
10:00 pm			Top Performers Recognition

ACCELERATE YOUR PERSONAL ACTIONS PLANNER (APAP)

My Schedule with (APAPs)		**Day/Date:** **Mission:**	
6:00 am			
7:00 am			
8:00 am			
9:00 am			
10:00 am			
11:00 am			
12:00 pm			**Accelerated Earnings Actions**
			Accelerated Coaching Activities with Downline
1:00 pm			Appointments & Interviews
			Accelerated Business Planning
2:00 pm			Collect & Deliver Customer Orders
			Conference Calls: Development & Recognition
3:00 pm			Downline Manager Reports & Planning
			Generate New Orders/Face-to-face & Online
4:00 pm			Follow-ups: Leads/No or Low –Orders
			Fundraising Presentations
5:00 pm			Listen to Skill Enhancing CDs
			New Recruits Training Contacts
6:00 pm			Online Training Courses
			Opportunity Presentations, Referrals
7:00 pm			Phone Dials for Referrals & Following Up
			Prospecting/Power Hour
8:00 pm			Product Promotions/Open House Selling
			Reading Business Development Books
9:00 pm			Sales Meeting/Unit Meeting/Other Meeting
			Seminar, Workshop, Retreat, Conference
10:00 pm			Top Performers Recognition

Accelerate your Personal Actions Planner (APAP)

My Schedule with (APAPs)		Day/Date: Mission:	
6:00 am			
7:00 am			
8:00 am			
9:00 am			
10:00 am			
11:00 am			
12:00 pm			**Accelerated Earnings Actions**
			Accelerated Coaching Activities with Downline
1:00 pm			Appointments & Interviews
			Accelerated Business Planning
2:00 pm			Collect & Deliver Customer Orders
			Conference Calls: Development & Recognition
3:00 pm			Downline Manager Reports & Planning
			Generate New Orders/Face-to-face & Online
4:00 pm			Follow-ups: Leads/No or Low –Orders
			Fundraising Presentations
5:00 pm			Listen to Skill Enhancing CDs
			New Recruits Training Contacts
6:00 pm			Online Training Courses
			Opportunity Presentations, Referrals
7:00 pm			Phone Dials for Referrals & Following Up
			Prospecting/Power Hour
8:00 pm			Product Promotions/Open House Selling
			Reading Business Development Books
9:00 pm			Sales Meeting/Unit Meeting/Other Meeting
			Seminar, Workshop, Retreat, Conference
10:00 pm			Top Performers Recognition

ACCELERATE YOUR PERSONAL ACTIONS PLANNER (APAP)

My Schedule with (APAPs)		Day/Date: Mission:	
6:00 am			
7:00 am			
8:00 am			
9:00 am			
10:00 am			
11:00 am			
12:00 pm			**Accelerated Earnings Actions**
			Accelerated Coaching Activities with Downline
1:00 pm			Appointments & Interviews
			Accelerated Business Planning
2:00 pm			Collect & Deliver Customer Orders
			Conference Calls: Development & Recognition
3:00 pm			Downline Manager Reports & Planning
			Generate New Orders/Face-to-face & Online
4:00 pm			Follow-ups: Leads/No or Low –Orders
			Fundraising Presentations
5:00 pm			Listen to Skill Enhancing CDs
			New Recruits Training Contacts
6:00 pm			Online Training Courses
			Opportunity Presentations, Referrals
7:00 pm			Phone Dials for Referrals & Following Up
			Prospecting/Power Hour
8:00 pm			Product Promotions/Open House Selling
			Reading Business Development Books
9:00 pm			Sales Meeting/Unit Meeting/Other Meeting
			Seminar, Workshop, Retreat, Conference
10:00 pm			Top Performers Recognition

Accelerate your Personal Actions Planner (APAP)

My Schedule with (APAPs)		Day/Date: Mission:	
6:00 am			
7:00 am			
8:00 am			
9:00 am			
10:00 am			
11:00 am			
12:00 pm			**Accelerated Earnings Actions**
			Accelerated Coaching Activities with Downline
1:00 pm			Appointments & Interviews
			Accelerated Business Planning
2:00 pm			Collect & Deliver Customer Orders
			Conference Calls: Development & Recognition
3:00 pm			Downline Manager Reports & Planning
			Generate New Orders/Face-to-face & Online
4:00 pm			Follow-ups: Leads/No or Low –Orders
			Fundraising Presentations
5:00 pm			Listen to Skill Enhancing CDs
			New Recruits Training Contacts
6:00 pm			Online Training Courses
			Opportunity Presentations, Referrals
7:00 pm			Phone Dials for Referrals & Following Up
			Prospecting/Power Hour
8:00 pm			Product Promotions/Open House Selling
			Reading Business Development Books
9:00 pm			Sales Meeting/Unit Meeting/Other Meeting
			Seminar, Workshop, Retreat, Conference
10:00 pm			Top Performers Recognition

Accelerate your Personal Actions Planner (APAP)

My Schedule with (APAPs)		**Day/Date:** **Mission:**	
6:00 am			
7:00 am			
8:00 am			
9:00 am			
10:00 am			
11:00 am			
12:00 pm			**Accelerated Earnings Actions**
			Accelerated Coaching Activities with Downline
1:00 pm			Appointments & Interviews
			Accelerated Business Planning
2:00 pm			Collect & Deliver Customer Orders
			Conference Calls: Development & Recognition
3:00 pm			Downline Manager Reports & Planning
			Generate New Orders/Face-to-face & Online
4:00 pm			Follow-ups: Leads/No or Low –Orders
			Fundraising Presentations
5:00 pm			Listen to Skill Enhancing CDs
			New Recruits Training Contacts
6:00 pm			Online Training Courses
			Opportunity Presentations, Referrals
7:00 pm			Phone Dials for Referrals & Following Up
			Prospecting/Power Hour
8:00 pm			Product Promotions/Open House Selling
			Reading Business Development Books
9:00 pm			Sales Meeting/Unit Meeting/Other Meeting
			Seminar, Workshop, Retreat, Conference
10:00 pm			Top Performers Recognition

Accelerate your Personal Actions Planner (APAP)

My Schedule with (APAPs)		Day/Date: Mission:	
6:00 am			
7:00 am			
8:00 am			
9:00 am			
10:00 am			
11:00 am			
12:00 pm			**Accelerated Earnings Actions**
			Accelerated Coaching Activities with Downline
1:00 pm			Appointments & Interviews
			Accelerated Business Planning
2:00 pm			Collect & Deliver Customer Orders
			Conference Calls: Development & Recognition
3:00 pm			Downline Manager Reports & Planning
			Generate New Orders/Face-to-face & Online
4:00 pm			Follow-ups: Leads/No or Low –Orders
			Fundraising Presentations
5:00 pm			Listen to Skill Enhancing CDs
			New Recruits Training Contacts
6:00 pm			Online Training Courses
			Opportunity Presentations, Referrals
7:00 pm			Phone Dials for Referrals & Following Up
			Prospecting/Power Hour
8:00 pm			Product Promotions/Open House Selling
			Reading Business Development Books
9:00 pm			Sales Meeting/Unit Meeting/Other Meeting
			Seminar, Workshop, Retreat, Conference
10:00 pm			Top Performers Recognition

Accelerate your Personal Actions Planner (APAP)

My Schedule with (APAPs)		**Day/Date:** **Mission:**	
6:00 am			
7:00 am			
8:00 am			
9:00 am			
10:00 am			
11:00 am			
12:00 pm			**Accelerated Earnings Actions**
			Accelerated Coaching Activities with Downline
1:00 pm			Appointments & Interviews
			Accelerated Business Planning
2:00 pm			Collect & Deliver Customer Orders
			Conference Calls: Development & Recognition
3:00 pm			Downline Manager Reports & Planning
			Generate New Orders/Face-to-face & Online
4:00 pm			Follow-ups: Leads/No or Low –Orders
			Fundraising Presentations
5:00 pm			Listen to Skill Enhancing CDs
			New Recruits Training Contacts
6:00 pm			Online Training Courses
			Opportunity Presentations, Referrals
7:00 pm			Phone Dials for Referrals & Following Up
			Prospecting/Power Hour
8:00 pm			Product Promotions/Open House Selling
			Reading Business Development Books
9:00 pm			Sales Meeting/Unit Meeting/Other Meeting
			Seminar, Workshop, Retreat, Conference
10:00 pm			Top Performers Recognition

ACCELERATE YOUR PERSONAL ACTIONS PLANNER (APAP)

My Schedule with (APAPs)		Day/Date: Mission:	
6:00 am			
7:00 am			
8:00 am			
9:00 am			
10:00 am			
11:00 am			
12:00 pm			**Accelerated Earnings Actions**
			Accelerated Coaching Activities with Downline
1:00 pm			Appointments & Interviews
			Accelerated Business Planning
2:00 pm			Collect & Deliver Customer Orders
			Conference Calls: Development & Recognition
3:00 pm			Downline Manager Reports & Planning
			Generate New Orders/Face-to-face & Online
4:00 pm			Follow-ups: Leads/No or Low –Orders
			Fundraising Presentations
5:00 pm			Listen to Skill Enhancing CDs
			New Recruits Training Contacts
6:00 pm			Online Training Courses
			Opportunity Presentations, Referrals
7:00 pm			Phone Dials for Referrals & Following Up
			Prospecting/Power Hour
8:00 pm			Product Promotions/Open House Selling
			Reading Business Development Books
9:00 pm			Sales Meeting/Unit Meeting/Other Meeting
			Seminar, Workshop, Retreat, Conference
10:00 pm			Top Performers Recognition

DREAM

Behind me is infinite power.

Before me is endless possibility.

Around me is boundless opportunity.

Why should I fear?

– Stella Stuart